The Gospel According To John 11-21 (Volume 2)

A unique verse-by-verse study of the Bible

Psalm 1:1-3: Blessed is the man that walketh not in the counsel of the ungodly, nor standeth in the way of sinners, nor sitteth in the seat of the scornful. But his delight is in the law of the LORD; and in his law doth he meditate day and night. And he shall be like a tree planted by the rivers of water, that bringeth forth his fruit in his season; his leaf also shall not wither; and whatsoever he doeth shall prosper.

Rev. James Bussard, B.B.S., M.Min.

All Scripture quotations are from the *Authorized (King James) Version of the Bible.*

All definitions, footnotes, and commentaries came from the following three sources:

      1. Strong's Exhaustive Concordance of the Bible

      2. Thayer's Greek Lexicon

      3. Webster's 1828 Dictionary

The definitions, footnotes, and commentaries provided are given as accurately as possible and are based upon the sources listed above. These studies do in no way proclaim themselves to be without error, even though the utmost care was taken to be accurate and faithful to the Word of God.

These studies were developed for a person using the *Authorized (King James) Version of the Bible.* A person that uses these studies with other versions may not be able to use them as efficiently.

Preface

I am the pastor of a small church in Mid-Maryland and have a young family. My wife and I regularly work with our children (especially with our oldest daughter, who is ten) to develop the habit of reading their Bibles every day. I preach and teach to our church family that we are given God's Word for a reason. It is only through regular study that we show ourselves approved unto God (*II Timothy 2:15*). It is only through faithful application of what we learn that our lives are successful in God's sight (*Joshua 1:8*). The Bible claims to be the only divine book on Earth that was given to us by God (*II Timothy 3:16*) to explain who He is, who we are, what are purpose is, who His Son, Jesus Christ, is, and much, much more. However, what good is the Bible to a person that does not know how to study it? What good is it to someone that does not know how to apply what they have learned? Generally, many believers get frustrated with churches, pastors, and the Bible in particular, because of these very occurrences. My daughter was not exempt.

My daughter, who has a heart for God and wants to know Him, was not getting anything out of her Bible reading. For instance, she would read in the *Psalms* and come up with, "God wants me to witness more," as an application. Now, that application is fine when offered up one time, but not when offered after reading every psalm! It was at that point the Holy Spirit revealed to me that she did not understand what she was reading and that I needed to do something about it; not just as a pastor, but as a father!

As a result, I began to look for studies that would help her understand her reading. After looking through the primary venues available to the average, American believer, I realized that there was nothing for her. Most Bible studies feed the individual what the teacher wants them to learn. Others do not encourage study or application of the scriptures. After a time, God impressed upon my heart to begin work on something that would allow a person to study the scriptures without frustration and know exactly what the Bible is talking about through any given chapter, which is the product you have before you. The purpose of these studies is fourfold:

1. To emphasize the need of Bible reading, study, and application in the Christian life

Many believers do not pick up their Bibles and/or are not encouraged to. It is a pastor's duty to take God's Word and explain it through preaching and teaching, especially to his congregation. These studies are set up so that a person can take a chapter (or portion of one) and study it day by day. This way the reader has a way to track their own progress through the Word of God, which is an encouragement in itself.

2. To explain the sometimes hard to understand language of the King James Version

I preach and teach from the King James Version of the scriptures and encourage our people to do the same. I have my reasons for doing so, which are not important to the purpose of these Bible studies. Though this translation is used exclusively in my preaching, I will be the first to admit that the language can be difficult to understand and define. The English Bible was translated from Hebrew and Greek, which not many people have studied today. However, many resources exist to help our study. It is my desire to take the language of the King James Version and define it, when needed, through those existing tools. This essentially takes out the middle-man and faithfully puts the foreign languages into modern English. Though I may commentate a little, the intent is not to make this into a commentary.

3. To encourage Christians to think about what God is saying to us through the scriptures

It is a pastor's duty to teach his congregation to have a personal relationship with God for themselves. Our Lord wants to know the individual believer personally. The Lord desires that all believers be thinking people. The only way to have a thinking person is to ask them questions. These Bible studies are setup to inspire the believer to consider the scriptures through simple questions and fill-in-the blanks. It does not have an agenda behind it other than this. It simply walks through the Bible and explains it.

4. To expose the believer to a growing relationship with God through the reading of the scriptures

Few believers have a relationship with God today. Their lack of Bible reading is part of that problem. If we read the scriptures every day, we will learn about God and how to be more like Him. If we apply the scriptures to our lives, we will grow closer to our Creator. These studies are but tools to help the average believer read their Bible and know their God better. This is applicable for every age and profitable for growth.

If God helps you to grow in your relationship with Him through these lessons, I hope you will share it with me (*HeritageParkPastor@Gmail.com*). Thank you for your interest in the scriptures. May God bless you as you walk with the Lord Jesus and learn of Him in His Word.

Best Regards,

Rev. James Bussard, B.B.S., M.Min.
Pastor of Heritage Park Baptist Church, Keymar, MD

Bible Study Questions (*John 11:1-57*)

Instructions: Pray that God will help you to understand this passage. Read through this Bible passage twice: once for reading and another time for understanding. After reading, consider and answer the questions listed below. Write down notes regarding anything else God spoke to you about.

1. As the chapter opens, what was the name of the man who was sick (*v.1*)[1]?

_____

2. Where did he live (*v.1*)[2]?

_____

3. Who else lived in this town (*v.1*)?

_____

4. What special thing did Mary do for the Lord Jesus (*v.2*)?

    a. She _____ the Lord with ointment

    b. She wiped His feet with her _____

5. What relationship did Mary have with Lazarus (*v.2*)?

_____

6. Because Lazarus was sick, what did these ladies do (*v.3*)?

_____

7. What did they say to Him (*v.3*)[3]?

_____

8. What did Jesus say, when He heard the message (*v.4*)[4]?

_____

9. Why did Jesus say that Lazarus was sick (*v.4*)?

    a. For the _____ of God

    b. That the Son of God might be _____ by it

10. What did Jesus have toward Martha, Mary, and Lazarus (*v.5*)[5]?

_____

11. What did Jesus do, when He heard that Lazarus was sick (*v.6*)[6]?

_____

---

[1] *John 11:1*: Lazarus means *one whom God helps* (Hebrew name: Eleazar)
[2] *John 11:1b*: Bethany means *House of dates* and was a village about two miles from Jerusalem
[3] *John 11:3*: The love mentioned here is *the sort that wishes one well and was founded in admiration and esteem*
[4] *John 11:4*: The death mentioned here is *physical death by which the soul leaves the body*
[5] *John 11:5*: The love mentioned here is *godly love*
[6] *John 11:6*: To abide means *to remain*

12. How long did He stay there (**v.6**)?

_____

13. After this time, what did He say to His disciples (*learners*) (**v.7**)?

_____

14. What title did Jesus' disciples use for Him (**v.8**)[7]?

_____

15. What was their reply to Jesus' instruction (**v.8**)?

      a. "The Jews of late (*at the present time*) sought to _____ you."

      b. "Will you _____ there again?"

16. How did Jesus answer them (**v.9**)?

      a. "Are there not twelve _____ in a day?"

      b. "If any man walks in the day, he does not _____..."

17. Why was this true (**v.9**)?

_____

18. What did He say happens to a person that walks in the night (**v.10**)?

_____

19. Why was this true (**v.10**)?

_____

20. Who did Jesus say that He was (**John 9:5**)?

_____

21. Will anyone stumble spiritually, if they have Jesus inside to help (**v.9-10**)?

_____

22. If a person does not have Jesus to help them, what are they walking in (**v.10; John 8:12**)?

_____

23. After Jesus said these things, what did He say to His disciples (**v.11**)?

      a. "Our friend Lazarus _____ (*to be dead*)..."

      b. "I go, that I may _____ him out of sleep."

24. How did the disciples reply (**v.12**)[8]?

_____

---

[7] **John 11:8**: Master means *teacher*
[8] **John 11:12**: This sleep is *calm, restful sleep*

25. What was Jesus really talking about (*v.13*)?

_____

26. What did His disciples think He was talking about (*v.13*)?

_____

27. What did Jesus make clear to His disciples (*v.14-15*)?

     a. "Lazarus is _____..."

     b. "I am _____ for your sakes that I was not there..." (*v.15*)

28. What was Jesus' intent for not being with Lazarus (*v.15*)?

_____

29. What did He say to them next (*v.15*)?

_____

30. Who spoke up in reply (*v.16*)?

_____

31. What was this man also called (*v.16*)[9]?

_____

32. What did he say to the rest of the disciples (*v.16*)?

_____

33. Why did he say this (*v.16*)?

_____

34. When Jesus came to Bethany, what did He find (*v.17*)?

_____

35. What city was Bethany nigh (close) to (*v.18*)?

_____

36. About how far was Bethany away from there (*v.18*)[10]?

_____

37. Who had come to Martha and Mary (*v.19*)?

_____

38. For what purpose had they done this (*v.19*)?

_____

_____

[9] *John 11:16*: Didymus means *twofold, twain, or twin*
[10] *John 11:18*: One furlong equals about 0.125 miles; Fifteen furlongs equal about 1.875 miles

39. Who heard that Jesus was coming (**v.20**)?

_____

40. What did she do as soon as she heard this (**v.20**)?

        a. She _____

        b. She _____ Him

41. What did Mary do (**v.20**)[11]?

_____

42. With what title did Martha address Jesus (**v.21**)?

_____

43. What did she say to Him (**v.21**)?

_____

44. What did she say that she knew (**v.22**)?

_____

_____

45. What was Jesus' reply (**v.23**)[12]?

_____

46. What was Martha's reply to Jesus' statement (**v.24**)?

_____

47. When did she think Lazarus would do this (**v.24**)[13]?

_____

48. What was Jesus' reply (**v.25**)[14] [15]?

_____

49. What did He say happened to those that believed in Him (*to believe in the nature and dignity of Jesus Christ*) (**v.25**)?

_____

50. Who did Jesus say would never die (*to be subject to eternal misery*) (**v.26**)

        a. Whoever _____ in Him

        b. Whoever _____ in Him

_____

[11] **John 11:20**: To sit still means *to be seated*

[12] **John 11:23**: To rise again means *to be resurrected from the dead*

[13] **John 11:24**: The last day speaks of *that time when the Messiah will come again and resurrect the bodies of the dead saints that sleep in Him* (cf. **I Thessalonians 4:13-18**)

[14] **John 11:25**: To be the resurrection means *to be the author of the resurrection from the dead*

[15] **John 11:26**: To be the life means *to be the giver of eternal life*

51. What question did Jesus ask Martha (*v.26*)?

_____

52. Do you believe that Jesus is the resurrection and the life (*v.25*)?

_____

53. Do you believe that, if you believe in Him that you will gain eternal life (*v.26*)?

_____

54. What was Martha's answer (*v.27*)?

    a. "Yes, _____..."

    b. "I believe that you are the _____ (*Messiah and Savior from sin*),

    the Son of God, which should come into the world."

55. What did she do, after she said these words (*v.28*)?

    a. She went her _____

    b. She _____ Mary secretly

56. What did she say to her (*v.28*)?

    a. "The _____ is come…"

    b. "The _____ calls for you."

57. What did Mary do as soon as she heard this (*v.29*)?

    a. She _____ (*to stand up*) quickly

    b. She _____ to Him

58. Where was Jesus, at this time (*v.30*)?

    a. He was not yet come into _____

    b. He was still in the place where _____ met Him

59. Who was with Mary in their house (*v.31*)?

_____

60. What were they doing there (*v.31*)?

_____

61. What did they do, when they saw her leave (*v.31*)?

_____

62. What did they say, as they did so (*v.31*)?

_____

63. What did Mary do, when she came to Jesus (*v.32*)?

      a. She _____ Him

      b. She _____ down at His feet

64. What did she say to Him (*v.32*)?

_____

65. What did Jesus see, as Mary spoke to Him (*v.33*)?

      a. Mary _____

      b. The Jews _____, which came with her

66. How did Jesus react to what He saw (*v.33*)?

      a. He _____ in the spirit (*to be very angry*)

      b. He was _____ (*to be afflicted with great sorrow*)

67. What did He say to the crowd (*v.34*)?

_____

68. What was their response (*v.34*)?

_____

69. How did Jesus react, when He reached the tomb (*v.35*)?

_____

70. What did the Jews say about Jesus, when they saw this (*v.36*)?

_____

71. What did some of the Jews say about Jesus' healing power (*v.37*)?

_____

_____

72. Because of these statements, what did Jesus do (*v.38*)?

      a. He _____ (*to be very angry*) within Himself

      b. He came to the _____

73. What is said about the tomb of Lazarus (*v.38*)?

      a. It was a _____

      b. A _____ lay (*to be placed*) upon it

74. What order did Jesus give to the people (*v.39*)?

_____

75. What was Lazarus' sister, Martha's reply (*v.39*)?

    a. "Lord, by this time he _____ (*to emit the smell of a*

    decaying corpse)…"

    b. "He has been _____ for four days."

76. What did Jesus remind Martha that He had said to her (*v.40*)?

_____

77. How do we see the glory of God (*v.40*)?

_____

78. What did the people do in response (*v.41*)?

_____

_____

79. What did Jesus do (*v.41*)?

_____

80. What did He say, in prayer to His Father in Heaven (*v.41-42*)?

    a. "I thank you that you have _____ me…"

    b. "I knew that you always _____ me…" (*v.42*)

    c. "Because of the _____ which stand by I said it…"

81. Why did Jesus say these words (*v.42*)?

_____

82. What did Jesus do, after He prayed (*v.43*)?

_____

83. What did He say (*v.43*)?

_____

84. What happened as a result (*v.44*)?

_____

85. How was Lazarus bound (*to bind or tie*) (*v.44*)?

    a. He was bound _____ and _____ with grave clothes

    b. His _____ was bound about with a napkin (*a handkerchief*)

86. What did Jesus command the people to do (*v.44*)?

    a. "_____ him."

    b. "Let him _____."

87. What happened to many of the Jews, when they saw what Jesus did (**v.45**)?

_____

88. What did some of the other Jews do (**v.46**)?

      a. They went their ways to the _____

      b. They told them the things _____ had done

89. What did the Pharisees and chief priests do in response (**v.47**)?

_____

90. What did they ask each other (**v.47**)[16]?

_____

91. Why were they distraught about what to do with Jesus (**v.47**)?

_____

92. What did they think would happen, if they left Him alone (**v.48**)?

      a. All the people would _____ on Him

      b. The _____ would come and take away their place (*the place in*

      which the nation of Israel inhabited)

      c. The _____ would come and take away their nation

93. Who spoke up in the midst of the council (**v.49**)?

_____

94. What was this man's position (**v.49**)?

_____

95. What did he say to the others (**v.49-50**)?

      a. "You all know _____ at all…"

      b. "You all do not consider that it is expedient (*profitable*) for us, that one man should

      _____ for the people…" (**v.50**)

      c. "You all do not consider that it is expedient for us, that the whole nation does not

      _____."

96. Was this man saying that he would give his own life for the people of Israel (**v.51**)?

_____

97. What had he prophesied during that same year (**v.51-52**)?

      a. That _____ would die for the nation of Israel

      b. That _____ would not die for Israel only (**v.52**)

_____

[16] *John 11:47*: What do we means "**What do we do?**"

12

98. What else did he say that Jesus would do (**v.52**)?

_____

_____

99. What did the religious leaders do from that day forward (**v.53**)?

_____

100. Because of this, what did Jesus not do anymore (**v.54**)?

_____

101. Where did He go instead (**v.54**)?

      a. He went into a country near the _____

      b. He went to a city called _____ (*a city several miles from Jerusalem*)

102. What did He do there (**v.54**)?

_____

103. What special event came to be close at hand (**v.55**)?

_____

104. What happened in Israel as a result (**v.55**)?

_____

105. Why did they do this (**v.55**)[17]?

_____

106. What did the people do, as they stood in the Temple (**v.56**)?

      a. They _____ for Jesus

      b. They _____ amongst themselves

107. What did they ask each other (**v.56**)?

      a. "What do you all _____?"

      b. "Will He come to the _____ (*a celebration for the Passover feast*) or not?"

108. Who had given a command to the people (**v.57**)?

_____

109. What was their command regarding Jesus (**v.57**)?

_____

110. Why did they want to know where Jesus was (**v.57**)[18]?

_____

---

[17] **John 11:55**: This was a ceremonial purification, where the people would cleanse themselves from sin by the means of prayers, abstinence, washings, and sacrifices at the Temple in Jerusalem

[18] **John 11:57**: To be taken means *to capture in order to imprison*

Meditation (What God Spoke to Me About):

_____

_____

_____

_____

_____

_____

_____

_____

Application (How I Can Apply What I Learned):

_____

_____

_____

_____

_____

_____

_____

_____

Memorization (How I Can Retain What I Read):

Suggestions: _John 11:9-10; 11:25-26; 11:35; 11:41-44_

_____

_____

_____

Assessment (How I Am Doing With My Application and Memorization):

_____

_____

_____

_____

_____

_____

Bible Study Questions (*John 12:1-50*)

Instructions: Pray that God will help you to understand this passage. Read through this Bible passage twice: once for reading and another time for understanding. After reading, consider and answer the questions listed below. Write down notes regarding anything else God spoke to you about.

1. What did Jesus do six days before the Passover (*v.1*)?

_____

2. Who lived in this town (*v.1*)?

_____

3. What had Jesus done for this person (*v.1*)?

_____

4. What did this family do for Jesus (*v.2*)?

     a. They made Him a _____

     b. Martha _____ (*to wait at the table and offer food or drink to the guests*)

5. What did Lazarus do (*v.2*)?

_____

6. What did Lazarus' sister, Mary do (*v.3*)[19]?

     a. She took a pound of _____ of spikenard

     b. She _____ the feet of Jesus

     c. She _____ His feet with her hair

7. What value did this ointment hold (*v.3*)?

_____

8. What happened to the house where this action was done (*v.3*)?

_____

9. Who spoke up about this action (*v.4*)?

_____

10. Whose son was this man (*v.4*)?

_____

11. What would this man do to Jesus (*v.4*)?

_____

_____

[19] **John 12:3**: Spikenard was taken from an East Indian plant, which yields a juice of delicious odor which the ancients used, often in ointment

12. What did he say should have been done with the ointment (*v.5*)?

_____

13. What did he say should have been done with the resulting money (*v.5*)?

_____

14. Why did he say this (*v.6*)?

      a. Not because he cared for the _____

      b. Because he was a _____

15. What was Judas' job among Jesus' disciples (*v.6*)?

      a. He had the _____ (*a purse to keep money in*)

      b. He _____ (*to carry*) what was put in it

16. What was Jesus' response to Judas' objection (*v.7*)?

      a. "Let her _____..."

      b. "Against the day of my _____ has she kept this."

17. Who did Jesus say they would always have with them (*v.8*)?

_____

18. Who did He say they would not always have with them (*v.8*)?

_____

19. Because of Jesus' work in Bethany, who knew that He was there (*v.9*)?

_____

20. Why did they come to Lazarus' house (*v.9*)?

      a. Not only for _____ sake

      b. That they might see _____ also

21. What special miracle had Jesus performed for Lazarus (*v.9*)?

_____

22. What did the chief priests consult together regarding Lazarus (*v.10*)?

_____

23. Why did they want to do this (*v.11*)?

      a. Because of Lazarus, many of the Jews went _____ (*to depart*)

      b. Because of Lazarus, many of the Jews _____ on Jesus

24. What happened the next day (*v.12*)[20]?

_____

_____

[20] *John 12:12*: This feast was one for the Passover and was held in Jerusalem

25. Why did they go there (**v.12**)?

_____

26. What did they do for Jesus (**v.13**)?

     a. They took branches of _____ trees

     b. They went to _____ Him

27. What did they cry (*to cry out*), as they went to Jesus (**v.13**)[21]?

_____

_____

28. What did Jesus find to sit upon (**v.14**)[22]?

_____

29. What did the scriptures say regarding this event (**v.15**)[23]?

_____

_____

30. Did Jesus' disciples understand what was happening at first (**v.16**)?

_____

31. What happened when Jesus was glorified (**v.16**)?

     a. His disciples remembered that these things were _____ of Him

     b. His disciples remembered that they had _____ these things to Him

32. Who bore record (*to testify*) that Jesus raised Lazarus from the dead, which caused this event (**v.17**)?

_____

33. Because of the testimony of these people, what happened (**v.18**)?

_____

34. Why did they do this (**v.18**)?

_____

35. Because the people did this, what did the Pharisees say among themselves (**v.19**)?

     a. "Do you all perceive how you _____ nothing (*to be of no use*)?"

     b. "Behold, the _____ is gone after Him (*to follow Jesus as a leader*)!"

_____

[21] **John 12:13**: Hosanna is *a favorable greeting toward a person*; in the case of the Messiah, this greeting was one that worshipped Him as being graceful and merciful; ready to forgive sins and bestow blessings

[22] **John 12:14**: An ass is *a donkey*

[23] **John 12:15**: Daughter of Zion refers to *the inhabitants of Jerusalem as a whole, where the Messiah would establish His Kingdom on Earth* (cf. **Zechariah 9:9**)

36. Who was present among the Jews (*v.20*)?

_____

37. Why were these people in Jerusalem (*v.20*)?

_____

38. Which disciple did these people come to (*v.21*)?

_____

39. What did the Greeks say to him (*v.21*)?

_____

40. What was this disciple's response (*v.22*)?

_____

41. What was that disciple's response (*v.22*)?

_____

42. What did Jesus say was come (*v.23*)[24]?

_____

43. What did He say would happen if a corn (*a grain*) of wheat did not fall to the ground and die (*v.24*)[25]?

_____

44. What did He say would happen if a corn of wheat does fall to the ground and die (*v.24*)?

_____

45. What did Jesus say about our lives (*v.25*)?

   a. "He that loves his life will _____ (*to destroy*) it…"

   b. "He that hates (*to detest*) his life will _____ (*to preserve*) it unto life eternal."

46. What did He say about those that wanted to serve Him (*v.26*)?

_____

47. Where did He say His servant would be (*v.26*)?

_____

48. What did He say His Father would do to His servant (*v.26*)[26]?

_____

49. What did Jesus say regarding His soul (*v.27*)?

_____

_____

[24] **John 12:23**: Hour refers *to a specific time*, instead of sixty minutes
[25] **John 12:24**: To abide means *to remain*
[26] **John 12:26**: To honor means *to reward Jesus' servants with honor and glory in the Kingdom*

50. What did He want to say to His Father (*v.27*)?

_____

51. Why did He not say these words (*v.27*)?

_____

52. What did He say instead to His Father (*v.28*)[27]?

_____

53. How did the Father reply from Heaven (*v.28*)?

     a. "I have _____ it…"

     b. "I will _____ it again."

54. What did the people that heard the voice say about it (*v.29*)?

     a. Some said that it _____

     b. Others said that an _____ spoke to Him

55. What did Jesus say to them about the voice (*v.30*)?

     a. It did not _____, because of Him

     b. It came for their _____

56. What did He say was come upon the world (*v.31*)[28]?

_____

57. What did He say about the prince of this world (*Satan*) (*v.31*)?

_____

58. What did He say would happen, if He was lifted up from the earth (*v.32*)[29]?

_____

59. Why did Jesus say this (*v.33*)?

_____

60. What had the people heard out of the Law about Christ (*the Messiah*) (*v.34*)?

_____

61. What did they ask Jesus (*v.34*)?

     a. "Why do you say, "The Son of _____ must be lifted up.'?"

     b. "Who is this Son of _____?"

_____

[27] **John 12:28**: To glorify means *to make the dignity and worth of someone to be known and acknowledged*
[28] **John 12:31**: This judgment was *the condemnatory sentence passed upon the world, in that it is convicted of sin and its power is broken*
[29] **John 12:32**: To be lifted up speaks of *Jesus being lifted up on the cross*

62. What was Jesus' response (*v.35*)[30]?

_____

63. What did He tell them to do (*v.35*)?

_____

64. Why did He tell them this (*v.35*)?

_____

65. What did He say about those that walk in darkness (*v.35*)?

_____

66. What did He tell them to do, while they had the light (*v.36*)?

_____

67. Why did He tell them to do this (*v.36*)?

_____

68. After He spoke these things, what did Jesus do (*v.36*)?

     a. He _____

     b. He _____ Himself from them

69. Even though Jesus performed many miracles before them, what was the Jews reaction to Him as a whole (*v.37*)?

_____

70. What prophet prophesied that this would happen (*v.38*)?

_____

71. What were the words of his prophecy (*v.38*)[31]?

     a. "Lord, who has believed our _____ (*the preaching of God's Word*)?"

     b. "Lord, to whom has the arm (*the power*) of the Lord been _____?"

72. Because of this prophecy, what could the Jews as a whole not do (*v.39*)?

_____

73. What were the words of another prophecy of Isaiah (*v.40*)?

     a. "He has _____ (*to be spiritually blind*) their eyes..."

     b. "He has _____ (*to be made callous*) their hearts..."

----

[30] **John 12:35**: Jesus is spoken of as the light; men that walk in the Light walk in Jesus' doctrine
[31] **John 12:38**: cf. *Isaiah 53:1*

74. Why did God do this (**v.40**)?

    a. "That they should not _____ (*to understand spiritual things*) with their eyes..."

    b. "That they should not _____ (*to understand spiritual things*)

    with their hearts..."

75. If the people of Israel would have understood and believed, what would have happened (**v.40**)?

    a. They would have been _____ (*to repent and return to God*)

    b. They would have been _____ (*to be saved from sin*) by God

76. When did Isaiah say these words (**v.41**)[32]?

    a. When he saw God's _____

    b. When he _____ of God

77. Despite this prophecy, what happened among many of the chief rulers (**v.42**)?

_____

78. What did they not do, because of the Pharisees (**v.42**)?

_____

79. Why did they not do this (**v.42-43**)?

    a. Lest they would have been put out of the _____

    b. They loved the _____ of men more than the _____

    of God (**v.43**)

80. Who did Jesus say those that believed on Him truly believed in (**v.44**)?

_____

81. What did He say about those that saw Him (**v.45**)?

_____

82. What did He say that He came as into the world (**v.46**)?

_____

83. Why did He do this (**v.46**)?

_____

84. What did Jesus say about those that heard His words and did not believe Him (**v.47**)?

_____

85. Why did He not do this (**v.47**)?

    a. He did not come to _____ (*to pass judgment upon*) the world

    b. He came to _____ (*to save from sin*) the world

_____

[32] *John 12:40*: cf. *Isaiah 6:1-10*

86. What does Jesus say will cause a person to be judged (*v.48*)?

     a. If they _____ Him

     b. If they do not _____ His words

87. What is it that will judge the unbeliever in the last day (the Day of Judgment) (*v.48*)?

_____

88. Why will this happen (*v.49*)?

_____

89. What did the Father, which sent Jesus to Earth, command Him regarding (*v.49*)?

     a. As to what He should _____

     b. As to what He should _____

90. What did Jesus say about the Father's command (*v.50*)[33]?

_____

91. Because this is true about the Father's command, what did Jesus testify to the Jews (*v.50*)?

_____

_____

---

[33] *John 12:50*: Commandment means *to charge one* (in this case: God the Father charged God the Son to speak of things regarding everlasting life to the world, which is what Jesus did)

Meditation (What God Spoke to Me About):

_____
_____
_____
_____
_____
_____
_____

Application (How I Can Apply What I Learned):

_____
_____
_____
_____
_____
_____
_____
_____

Memorization (How I Can Retain What I Read):

Suggestions: *John 12:7-8; 12:24-26; 12:35-36; 12:44-50*

_____
_____
_____
_____

Assessment (How I Am Doing With My Application and Memorization):

_____
_____
_____
_____
_____
_____

Bible Study Questions (*John 13:1-38*)

Instructions: Pray that God will help you to understand this passage. Read through this Bible passage twice: once for reading and another time for understanding. After reading, consider and answer the questions listed below. Write down notes regarding anything else God spoke to you about.

1. During what time does this chapter open (*v.1*)?

     a. Before the feast of the _____

     b. When Jesus knew that His _____ (*a period of time*) was come

2. What would happen during this period of time to Jesus (*v.1*)?

_____

3. Where would He go to (*v.1*)?

_____

4. Who did He love (*to have godly love towards*) (*v.1*)?

_____

5. How long did He love them (*v.1*)[34]?

_____

6. What had ended (*v.2*)[35]?

_____

7. What had the Devil done to Judas Iscariot (*v.2*)?

_____

8. What did Jesus know about the situation (*v.3*)?

     a. That the Father had _____ (*to deliver to one's power*) all things into

     His hands

     b. That He was _____ from God

     c. That He _____ to God

9. Knowing this, what did Jesus do (*v.4*)[36] [37]?

     a. He _____ (*to rise from reclining*) from supper

     b. He laid aside (*to wear no longer*) His _____

     c. He took a _____ (*a linen apron used by servants*)

     d. He _____ Himself

---

[34] *John 13:1*: To the end means *to the very last*
[35] *John 13:2*: Supper means *the formal meal that normally occurred at evening*
[36] *John 13:4*: Garment means *an outer garment*
[37] *John 13:4*: To gird means *to bind or wrap around oneself*

10. What did Jesus do after He did these things (**v.5**)?

       a. He poured _____ into a basin

       b. He began to _____ the disciples' feet

       c. He _____ them with the towel He was girded with

11. Which disciple did Jesus eventually come to (**v.6**)?

_____

12. What did this man ask Him (**v.6**)?

_____

13. What was Jesus' answer to him (**v.7**)?

       a. "What I do you do not _____ now…"

       b. "What I do you will _____ hereafter."

14. What was Peter's reply (**v.8**)?

_____

15. How did Jesus respond to him (**v.8**)[38]?

_____

16. What was Peter's response (**v.9**)?

       a. "Lord, not my _____ only…"

       b. "Also my _____ and my _____."

17. What did Jesus answer regarding those that were washed (*to be cleansed of sin*) (**v.10**)[39]?

       a. "He does not need save (*other than*) to wash His _____…"

       b. "Every whit (*part*) of him is _____ (*pure*)."

18. What did Jesus then say about His disciples (**v.10**)?

_____

19. Why did He say this about them (**v.11**)?

_____

20. What did Jesus do after washing the disciples' feet (**v.12**)?

       a. He took His _____

       b. He _____ down again

---

[38] *John 13:8*: To have no part means *to have no fellowship* (in this case: with Jesus)

[39] *John 13:10* (lit.): "**He whose innermost nature has been renovated does not need radical renewal, but only to be cleansed from every several fault into which he may fall through contact with the unrenewed world.**" (speaking of a regular purging of sin in order to maintain good fellowship with Jesus Christ (cf. *1 John 1:9*))

21. What did He then ask His disciples (*v.12*)?

_____

22. What did He say that His disciples called Him (*v.13*)[40] [41]?

_____

23. What did He have to say about that (*v.13*)?

_____

24. Why was this true (*v.13*)?

_____

25. If Jesus was these things to His disciples and washed their feet, what did He tell them to do (*v.14*)?

_____

26. Why were they to do this (*v.15*)?

_____

_____

27. What did Jesus then say to His disciples (*v.16*)?

    a. "The _____ is not greater than His lord..."

    b. "He that is _____ is not greater than He that sent Him."

28. What did He say would happen, if the disciples knew these things and did them (*v.17*)?

_____

29. Was Jesus speaking about all of His disciples (*v.18*)?

_____

30. What did He know about His disciples (*v.18*)?

_____

31. What was the Scripture that He said needed to be fulfilled (*v.18*)[42] [43]?

_____

_____

32. Why did Jesus tell the disciples about this prophecy before it came to pass (*v.19*)?

_____

33. What did He say about those that received whomever He sent (*v.20*)?

_____

---

[40] *John 13:13*: Master means *teacher*

[41] *John 13:13*: Lord means *one who possesses a thing* (in this case: Jesus owns His disciples as their Lord)

[42] *John 13:18*: cf. *Psalm 41:9*

[43] *John 13:18*: To lift up the heel means *to injure a person by means of trickery*

34. What did He say about those that received Him (**v.20**)?

_____

35. What happened after Jesus said these things (**v.21**)?

        a. He was _____ (*to be affected with great sorrow*) in spirit

        b. He _____ (*to bear witness*)

36. What did He then tell his disciples (**v.21**)?

_____

37. How did the disciples react (**v.22**)?

        a. They _____ at one another

        b. They _____ (*to be at a loss*) of whom He spoke

38. Who was leaning on Jesus' bosom (**v.23**)[44] [45] [46]?

_____

39. Because of this man's positioning to Jesus, who beckoned to this man (**v.24**)?

_____

40. What did he beckon for him to do (**v.24**)?

_____

_____

41. What did this disciple do (**v.25**)?

        a. He laid (*to fall back upon*) on _____ breast

        b. He asked Him, "_____, who is it?"

42. What was Jesus' answer (**v.26**)[47]?

_____

43. Who did He give the sop to, when He had dipped it (**v.26**)?

_____

44. What happened to this man, after Jesus gave him the sop (**v.27**)[48]?

_____

45. What did Jesus say to this man (**v.27**)?

_____

_____

[44] **John 13:23**: To lean on Jesus' bosom means *to recline at the table so that his head covered Jesus' bosom, because Jesus was the one next to him* (the custom of that time was not to sit at a meal, but to recline)
[45] **John 13:23** (lit.): "**Now there was one reclining close to Jesus one of His disciples, whom He loved.**"
[46] **John 13:23**: John the Apostle often used the title "The Disciple whom Jesus loved" to refer to himself
[47] **John 13:26**: A sop means *a morsel of food*
[48] **John 13:27**: To enter in means *to take demonic possession of one* (in this case: Satan possessed Judas Iscariot)

46. Did anyone know why Jesus said this to Judas (*v.28*)?

_____

47. What did some of them think Jesus had said to him (*v.29*)?

     a. To _____ the things they had need of against (*for*) the feast

     b. That he should give something to the _____

48. Why did they think Jesus might have said these things (*v.29*)?

_____

49. After Judas received the sop, what did he do (*v.30*)?

_____

50. During what time of day did he do this (*v.30*)?

_____

51. Because Judas did this, what did Jesus say to the remaining disciples (*v.31*)?

     a. "Now is the Son of Man _____ (*to cause the dignity and worth*

     of someone to be made known)..."

     b. "God is _____ in Him."

52. What did He say would happen, if God was glorified in Him (*v.32*)?

     a. God will _____ Him in Himself

     b. God will straightway (*immediately*) _____ Him

53. What did Jesus call His disciples (*v.33*)[49]?

_____

54. What did He say about His time with them (*v.33*)?

_____

55. What did He say they would do (*v.33*)?

_____

56. What had He said to the Jews and now said to them (*v.33*)?

_____

57. What did Jesus give to His disciples (*v.34*)[50]?

_____

---

[49] **John 13:33**: Little children was *a term of endearment given from a teacher to his students*
[50] **John 13:34**: A commandment is *a command or order*

58. What was it (**v.34**)[51]?

     a. "That you all _____ (*to have godly love toward*) one another; as I have

     _____ you..."

     b. "That you all also _____ one another."

59. How did Jesus say that all men would know that they were His disciples (*learners*) (**v.35**)?

_____

60. How will all men know that we are Jesus' disciples (**v.35**)?

_____

61. Who spoke up, after Jesus said this (**v.36**)?

_____

62. What did he ask the Lord (**v.36**)?

_____

63. What was Jesus' answer (**v.36**)?

     a. "Where I go, you cannot _____ me now..."

     b. "You will _____ me afterwards."

64. What did Peter then ask Jesus (**v.37**)?

_____

65. What did he say that he would do for Jesus (**v.37**)?

_____

66. What was Jesus' reply (**v.38**)?

_____

67. What did He prophesy would happen to Peter (**v.38**)[52] [53]?

_____

---

[51] **John 13:34**: This love is *godly love that chooses to love a person no matter what happens*
[52] **John 13:38**: A cock is *a rooster*
[53] **John 13:38**: Thrice means *three times*

Meditation (What God Spoke to Me About):

_____

_____

_____

_____

_____

_____

_____

Application (How I Can Apply What I Learned):

_____

_____

_____

_____

_____

_____

_____

_____

Memorization (How I Can Retain What I Read):

Suggestions: *John 13:1-5; 13:12-17; 13:34-35*

_____

_____

_____

Assessment (How I Am Doing With My Application and Memorization):

_____

_____

_____

_____

_____

_____

Bible Study Questions (*John 14:1-31*)

Instructions: Pray that God will help you to understand this passage. Read through this Bible passage twice: once for reading and another time for understanding. After reading, consider and answer the questions listed below. Write down notes regarding anything else God spoke to you about.

1. As Jesus continues His message to His disciples, what does He command them to do (*v.1*)[54]?

_____

2. If they believed in God, what else did they need to do (*v.1*)[55]?

_____

3. What did Jesus say was in His Father's house (*speaking of Heaven*) (*v.2*)[56]?

_____

4. What did He say that He would have told the disciples (*v.2*)?

_____

5. What did He say that He was going to go do (*v.2*)[57]?

_____

6. If Jesus was going to do those things, what else did He say that He would do (*v.3*)?

    a. "I will _____ again…"

    b. "I will _____ you unto myself."

7. Why did He promise to do this (*v.3*)?

_____

8. What else did Jesus tell His disciples (*v.4*)?

    a. "You all _____ to where I go…"

    b. "You all _____ the way (*path*)."

9. Who spoke up amongst the disciples (*v.5*)?

_____

10. What did he ask Jesus (*v.5*)?

    a. "Lord, we do not _____ to where you go…"

    b. "Lord, how can we _____ the way?"

---

[54] *John 14:1*: To be troubled means *to be filled with fear and dread*
[55] *John 14:1*: To believe means *an acknowledgment joined with absolute trust* (in this case: in God and Christ)
[56] *John 14:2*: Mansion means *a dwelling place or abode*
[57] *John 14:2*: To prepare means *to get everything ready*

11. What was Jesus' answer to Thomas (*v.6*)?

    a. "I am the _____ (*the path through which all must pass that seek*

    fellowship with God)…"

    b. "I am the _____ (*the embodiment and summation of all truth*)…"

    c. "I am the _____ (*the giver of eternal life*)

12. How did He say that a man comes to the Father (*v.6*)?

_____

13. Did Jesus say that He was one way to Heaven or the only way to Heaven (*v.6*)?

_____

14. How can a person be with God in Heaven, without approaching through Jesus (*v.6*)?

_____

15. If Jesus' disciples knew Him, who else should they have known (*v.7*)?

_____

16. What did Jesus say would happen to His disciples from that point forward (*v.7*)?

    a. They would _____ the Father

    b. They had _____ the Father

17. What other disciple spoke up about Jesus' statements (*v.8*)?

_____

18. What did he say (*v.8*)?

    a. "Lord, _____ (*to render one to be visible*) us the Father…"

    b. "It _____ (*to make one to be content*) us."

19. What did Jesus ask him in return (*v.9*)?

    a. "Have I been so long _____ with you?"

    b. "Yet, have you not _____ me, Philip?"

20. Who did He say the disciples had seen, because they saw Him (*v.9*)?

_____

21. Because of this truth, what did He ask the disciples (*v.9*)?

_____

22. What else did Jesus ask His disciples about this subject (*v.10*)?

    a. "Do you not _____ that I am in the Father?"

    b. "Do you not _____ that the Father is in me?"

23. What did He tell them about the words that He said to them (*v.10*)?

_____

24. Who did He say did the works (*v.10*)?

_____

25. What did Jesus tell His disciples to believe (*v.11*)?

      a. That He was in the _____

      b. That the _____ was in Him

26. If nothing else, why did He tell them to believe His words (*v.11*)?

_____

27. What did Jesus then say to His disciples about those that believed in Him (*v.12*)?

      a. That the _____ that He did, they would do also

      b. That they would do greater _____ than Jesus did

28. Why would this be true (*v.12*)?

_____

29. Because Jesus would do this, what did He say the disciples could then expect (*v.13*)?

_____

30. Why would this happen (*v.13*)?

_____

31. Again, what promise did Jesus give to His disciples (*v.14*)?

_____

32. What is the key to seeing our prayers answered (*v.13-14*)?

_____

33. What did Jesus then say His disciples would do, to prove they loved Him (*v.15*)?

_____

34. What did He promise to do, if they did this (*v.16*)[58]?

_____

35. What did He promise the Father would do, when He did this (*v.16*)[59]?

_____

36. Why would He do this (*v.16*)[60]?

_____

_____

[58] *John 14:16*: To pray means *to request*
[59] *John 14:16*: Comforter means *helper or assistant*
[60] *John 14:16*: To abide means *to remain*

37. Who is this Comforter (**v.17**)?

_____

38. What is unique about the Comforter (**v.17**)?

_____

39. Why is this true (**v.17**)?

    a. Because the world does not _____ (*to not have spiritual eyes with which*

    to see the Spirit) Him

    b. Because the world does not _____ Him

40. What did Jesus say to the disciples about their relationship with the Comforter (**v.17**)?

_____

41. Why was this true (**v.17**)?

    a. Because He _____ (*to be present to help*) with them

    b. Because He would be _____ them

42. What else did He promise them, regarding the Comforter (**v.18**)?

    a. "I will not leave you _____ (*of those without a teacher, guide,*

    or guardian)…"

    b. "I will _____ (*to exert His power through the power of the Spirit*) to you."

43. What did Jesus say would happen after a little while (**v.19**)?

    a. The world would not _____ Him

    b. However, His disciples would _____ Him

44. What would happen to His disciples, because Jesus lived (**v.19**)?

_____

45. What did He say would happen to His disciples at that day (*the time where Jesus is revealed as the Messiah*) (**v.20**)?

    a. They would know that He was in His _____

    b. They would know that they were in _____

    c. They would know that _____ was in them

46. Who did Jesus say it was that loved Him (**v.21**)?

    a. Those that _____ (*to hold fast to or keep*) His commandments

    b. Those that _____ (*to observe*) His commandments

47. What did He say about those that loved Him (**v.21**)?

      a. They will be _____ by the Father

      b. Jesus will _____ them

      c. Jesus will _____ (*to present Himself to one's sight*) Himself to them

48. What other disciple spoke to Jesus about His words (**v.22**)?

_____

49. Was this Judas Iscariot (**v.22**)?

_____

50. What did He ask Jesus (**v.22**)?

_____

_____

51. What was Jesus' answer to Judas (**v.23**)[61]?

_____

52. What did He say happened to all those that kept His words (**v.23**)?

      a. "My _____ will love him…"

      b. "We will _____ (*to come in the power of the Spirit of God*) unto him…"

      c. "We will make our _____ (*to dwell spiritually within*) with him."

53. What did Jesus say about those that did not love Him (**v.24**)?

_____

54. Whose words did He say that He was giving to the disciples (**v.24**)?

_____

55. Did Jesus speak these things to His disciples, while He was still with them (**v.25**)?

_____

56. Who did He say would help them, when He was gone (**v.26**)?

_____

57. What is another name for this Person (**v.26**)?

_____

58. Who would send this Person (**v.26**)?

_____

59. How would He be sent (**v.26**)?

_____

_____

[61] **John 14:23**: To keep means *to observe*

60. What did Jesus say the Comforter would do on Earth (**v.26**)?

      a. He would _____ them all things

      b. He would _____ all things to their remembrance (*to cause one*

      to remember)

61. What things would the Spirit teach and remind the disciples of (**v.26**)?

_____

62. What did Jesus say that He was leaving with the disciples (**v.27**)[62]?

_____

63. What did He say that He was giving to the disciples (**v.27**)?

_____

64. Is this anything that the world can give (**v.27**)?

_____

65. What command did Jesus give to His disciples, because of this (**v.27**)[63] [64]?

_____

66. What did He say that the disciples had heard Him say to them (**v.28**)?

      a. "I _____ away…"

      b. "I will _____ again to you."

67. What else did Jesus say His disciples would do, if they loved Him (**v.28**)?

_____

68. Why would they do this (**v.28**)?

      a. Because He went to His _____

      b. Because His _____ was greater than He

69. Why did He tell the disciples that these things would happen (**v.29**)?

_____

70. What did Jesus say would happen after that period of time (**v.30**)?

_____

71. Why would this happen (**v.30**)?

      a. "The _____ of this world (*the devil*) comes…"

      b. "The _____ of this world has nothing in (*to have no power over*) me."

---

[62] **John 14:27**: This peace is *that which comes from the certainty of a soul's salvation; therefore having no fear of judgment of sin from God and being content with the earthly lot given by God*

[63] **John 14:27**: To be troubled means *to strike one's spirit with fear or dread*

[64] **John 14:27**: To be afraid means *to be timid*

72. If not because of Satan's power, why did Jesus do the work He did (*v.31*)?

    a. So that the world would know that He loved the _____

    b. Because the _____ gave Him the command to do the work

73. What command did Jesus then give to His disciples (*v.31*)?

    a. "_____ (*to rise from reclining*)..."

    b. "Let us _____ hence (*from this place*)."

Meditation (What God Spoke to Me About):

_____

_____

_____

_____

_____

_____

_____

Application (How I Can Apply What I Learned):

_____

_____

_____

_____

_____

_____

_____

_____

Memorization (How I Can Retain What I Read):

Suggestions: *John 14:1-4; 14:6; 14:12-18; 14:23-24; 14:25-28*

_____

_____

_____

Assessment (How I Am Doing With My Application and Memorization):

_____

_____

_____

_____

_____

_____

Bible Study Questions (*John 15:1-27*)

Instructions: Pray that God will help you to understand this passage. Read through this Bible passage twice: once for reading and another time for understanding. After reading, consider and answer the questions listed below. Write down notes regarding anything else God spoke to you about.

1. Who did Jesus say that He was (*v.1*)[65]?

_____

2. Who did He say that His Father was (*v.1*)[66]?

_____

3. What does the Father do to every branch in Jesus that does not bear fruit (*v.2*)[67] [68]?

_____

4. What does the Father do to every branch in Jesus that does bear fruit (*v.2*)[69]?

_____

5. Why does He do this (*v.2*)?

_____

6. How did Jesus say His disciples were made clean (*v.3*)[70]?

_____

7. What did He command them to do (*v.4*)?

    a. "_____ (*to remain*) in me…"

    b. "I will _____ (*to remain*) in you."

8. How does the branch bear fruit of itself (*v.4)?*

_____

9. How does Jesus say the believer bears fruit (*v.4*)?

_____

10. Can the branch bear fruit, if it does not abide in the vine (*v.4*)?

_____

_____

[65] *John 15:1*: Jesus calls Himself the vine, which is a spiritual picture of the Lord Jesus as the vine, because the vine imparts sap and productiveness to its branches; even as Christ imparts divine strength and life to His followers
[66] *John 15:1*: A husbandman is *a vine-dresser*
[67] *John 15:2*: To take away means *to cut off* (in this case: cutting the branch (the believer) off the vine (Jesus))
[68] *John 15:2*: To bear fruit means *to bring forth works for the propagation of the Gospel and its furtherance in the souls of men*
[69] *John 15:2*: To purge means *to cleanse from filth and impurity*
[70] *John 15:3*: To be made clean means *to be cleansed by pruning and so fitted to bear fruit*

11. If we do not abide in Jesus, can we bear fruit for Him (*v.4*)?

_____

12. Who does Jesus say that He is (*v.5*)?

_____

13. Who does He say that those that believe in Him are (*v.5*)?

_____

14. What happens to a person that abides in Christ (*v.5*)?

_____

15. Why does this happen (*v.5*)[71]?

_____

16. What happens to those that do not abide in Christ (*v.6*)?

       a. He is _____ forth (*to be thrown away*) as a branch

       b. He is _____ (*to become dried up*)

17. What does Jesus say that men do to such people (*v.6*)[72]?

       a. They _____ them

       b. They cast them into the _____

       c. They _____ them

18. Is Jesus speaking literally or figuratively regarding the vine and branches (*v.1-6*)?

_____

19. What does Jesus say will happen, if we abide in Him and His words (*v.7*)?

       a. We can _____ (*to ask for oneself in prayer*) what we will (*to desire*)

       b. It will be _____ unto us

20. How is God the Father glorified (*v.8*)?

_____

21. If we do this, what does Jesus call us (*v.8*)[73]?

_____

22. What did God the Father exhibit to Jesus Christ (*v.9*)?

_____

_____

[71] *John 15:5*: To do nothing means *to not have the power to do anything*
[72] *John 15:6*: The picture presented is the judgment of God upon the believer that will not abide in Christ; they do not have God's power and blessing and are useless and withered; they are only good to be burned (cf. *Matt. 5:13*)
[73] *John 15:8*: A disciple is *one who studies under another*

23. What did Jesus exhibit to His disciples in turn (*v.9*) [74]?

_____

24. Because of this, what did He command them to do (*v.9*)[75]?

_____

25. How did Jesus say that we can abide in (*to hold fast to*) His love (*v.10*)?

_____

26. What did He do as an example to His disciples (*v.10*)?

      a. He _____ His Father's commandments

      b. He abided in His _____

27. Why did Jesus tell His disciples these things (*v.11*)?

      a. That His _____ might remain in (*to not depart from*) them

      b. That their _____ might be full (*to be made complete and perfect*)

28. What was Jesus' commandment to His disciples (*v.12*)?

_____

29. Why did He say they should obey this command (*v.12*)?

_____

30. What does Jesus say is the greatest way to show love (*v.13*)?

_____

31. What did He say that His disciples could be (*v.14*)?

_____

32. How could this happen (*v.14*)?

_____

33. From that time forward, what did Jesus no longer call His disciples (*v.15*)[76]?

_____

34. Why did He no longer call them this (*v.15*)?

_____

35. What did Jesus choose to call His disciples instead (*v.15*)[77]?

_____

---

[74] *John 15:9*: The love presented here is *godly love*, which is unconditional love
[75] *John 15:10*: To continue means *to hold fast to a thing* (in this case: the love of Christ)
[76] *John 15:15*: Servant means *slave*
[77] *John 15:15*: Friend means *an associate or partner* (the opposite of slave)

36. Why did He call them this (*v.15*)?

_____

_____

37. Did Jesus say that they had chosen (*to choose out for oneself*) Him (*v.16*)?

_____

38. What did He say that He had done (*v.16*)?

      a. He had _____ (*to choose out for oneself*) them

      b. He had _____ (*to appoint*) them

39. What had He chosen and appointed them to do (*v.16*)?

      a. That they should _____

      b. That they should bring forth _____ (*to accomplish much for the*

      propagation of the Gospel and doing the work of Christ)

      c. That their _____ should remain (*to not perish*)

40. Why did Jesus say that they should do this (*v.16*)?

_____

_____

41. When we ask the Father for something, how should we ask (*v.16*)?

_____

42. When we do the work of the Father and ask this way, what will happen (*v.16*)[78]?

_____

43. Should we expect God to answer our prayers, if we do not do His work (*v.16*)?

_____

44. Should we expect God to answer our prayers, if we do not pray through Jesus (*v.16*)?

_____

45. Why did Jesus command these things to His disciples (*v.17*)?

_____

46. What did He say the disciples could know, if the world (*the ungodly multitude*) hated them (*v.18*)?

_____

47. What did He say would happen, if the disciples were of the world (*v.19*)?

_____

_____

[78] **John 15:16**: To give it you means *to grant it to you*

48. Why did Jesus say that the world (*the ungodly multitude*) would hate them (**v.19**)?

      a. Because they were not of (*to be part of*) the _____

      b. Because He chose them out of the _____

49. What did Jesus tell the disciples to remember (**v.20**)?

_____

50. What words were these (**v.20**)?

_____

51. What did Jesus say would happen to them, if the world persecuted Him (**v.20**)?

_____

52. What did He say would happen, if the world kept (*to observe*) His saying (*word*) (**v.20**)?

_____

53. Do you think that, if you do Jesus' work and follow Him that the world may persecute you (**v.20**)?

_____

54. Why would the world do these things to Jesus' disciples (**v.21**)?

      a. Because of His _____ sake

      b. Because they did not _____ He that sent Him

55. How did Jesus reveal sin to the world (**v.22**)?

      a. He _____ to the world (*the ungodly multitude*)

      b. He _____ to the world

56. Because Jesus did this, what did the world not have anymore (**v.22**)[79]?

_____

57. What did He say about those that hated Him (**v.23**)?

_____

58. What did He say that He had done among the world (**v.24**)?

_____

59. Had any other man done works like Jesus before (**v.24**)?

_____

60. Because of these works, what did He reveal to the world (*the ungodly multitude*) (**v.24**)?

_____

---

[79] **John 15:22**: A cloke means *an alleged reason or pretext*

61. At that point in His ministry, what did Jesus say about the world (**v.24**)?

    a. They had _____ both Him and His Father

    b. They _____ both Him and His Father

62. Why did this have to happen (**v.25**)?

_____

63. Where was this word written (**v.25**)?

_____

64. What did it say (**v.25**)?

_____

65. Who did Jesus say was coming (**v.26**)[80]?

_____

66. Who would send this Person (**v.26**)?

_____

67. What is another name for this Person (**v.26**)?

_____

68. Where did this Person proceed from (**v.26**)?

_____

69. What did Jesus say this Person would do (**v.26**)[81]?

_____

70. What did He say that His disciples would do with the Comforter (**v.27**)?

_____

71. Why would they do this (**v.27**)?

_____

---

[80] **John 15:26**: Comforter means *assistant or helper*
[81] **John 15:26**: To testify means *to bear witness*

Meditation (What God Spoke to Me About):

_____

_____

_____

_____

_____

_____

_____

Application (How I Can Apply What I Learned):

_____

_____

_____

_____

_____

_____

_____

_____

Memorization (How I Can Retain What I Read):

Suggestions: *John 15:1-5; 15:8-14; 15:17; 15:26-27*

_____

_____

_____

Assessment (How I Am Doing With My Application and Memorization):

_____

_____

_____

_____

_____

_____

_____

Bible Study Questions (*John 16:1-33*)

Instructions: Pray that God will help you to understand this passage. Read through this Bible passage twice: once for reading and another time for understanding. After reading, consider and answer the questions listed below. Write down notes regarding anything else God spoke to you about.

1. As Jesus continued His sermon, why had He said these things to His disciples (**v.1**)[82] [83]?

_____

2. What else did He say would happen to them (**v.2**)[84]?

_____

3. What else was coming (**v.2**)[85]?

_____

_____

4. Why would the world do these things to the disciples (**v.3**)?

    a. Because they have not _____ (*to know the nature of, instead of*

    having false wisdom about) the Father

    b. Because they have not _____ Jesus Christ

5. Why did Jesus tell the disciples about these things (**v.4**)?

_____

_____

6. Why did Jesus not tell the disciples about these things at the beginning of His ministry (**v.4**)?

_____

7. What did He say He was going to do at that time (**v.5**)?

_____

8. Where was He going to (**v.5**)?

_____

9. What did none of the disciples ask Him (**v.5**)?

_____

---

[82] *John 16:1*: In the previous chapter, Jesus explained the importance of abiding in Him, bearing fruit as they did His work, that they were chosen by Him to do His work, and that the world as a whole would hate them; just as they hated Jesus Christ

[83] *John 16:1*: To be offended means *to cause someone to distrust and desert one they ought to be trusting and following* (in this case: Jesus Christ)

[84] *John 16:2*: To be put out means *to be excommunicated*

[85] *John 16:2*: To do God service means *to offer a sacrifice to God as an act of worship*

10. Because of Jesus' words, how did His disciples react (**v.6**)?

_____

11. Despite their sorrow, what did Jesus say that He told them (**v.7**)?

_____

12. What did He say about what He told them (**v.7**)[86]?

_____

13. Why was this true (**v.7**)[87]?

_____

_____

14. What would happen, if Jesus departed (**v.7**)?

_____

15. What did Jesus say the Comforter would do, when He came (**v.8**)?

    a. He would reprove (*to convict in order to shame*) the world of _____ (*of the sinfulness of mankind*)

    b. He would reprove the world of _____ (*of the purity and sinlessness of Jesus Christ*)

    c. He would reprove the world of _____ (*of divine judgment passed upon sin*)

16. Why did the Comforter need to reprove the world of its sin (**v.9**)?

_____

17. Why did the Comforter need to reprove the world to reveal Jesus' righteousness (**v.10**)?

    a. Because Jesus was going to His _____

    b. Because Jesus' disciples would _____ Him no more

18. Why did the Comforter need to reprove the world to reveal God's judgment (**v.11**)[88] [89]?

_____

19. How much more did Jesus have to say to His disciples (**v.12**)?

_____

_____

[86] **John 16:7**: Expedient means *profitable*
[87] **John 16:7**: Comforter means *assistant* (referring to the Spirit of God)
[88] **John 16:11**: The prince of this world refers to *Satan*
[89] **John 16:11**: The prince of this world being judged refers to *Jesus' victorious work rendering the work of Satan to be evident to those that believe; putting an end to his power to dominate and destroy mankind through sin*

20. Why did He not say them to them (*v.12*)[90]?

_____

21. Who did Jesus say was coming (*v.13*)?

_____

22. What is another name for this Person (*v.7*)?

_____

23. What did Jesus say this Person would do for the disciples (*v.13*)?

_____

24. Why would this Person do this (*v.13*)?

_____

25. How would this Person operate (*v.13*)?

      a. Whatever He heard, He would _____

      b. He would _____ (*to disclose to*) them things to come

26. What else would this Person do (*v.14*)?

_____

27. Why would He do this (*v.14*)[91]?

      a. He would _____ of Jesus (*that which Jesus possesses*)

      b. He would _____ (*to disclose*) it to the disciples

28. What did Jesus say about all things the Father had (*v.15*)?

_____

29. How much of what the Father has does Jesus have access to (*v.15*)?

_____

30. Because of this truth, what did Jesus say to His disciples (*v.15*)?

      a. That the Spirit of truth would _____ of Jesus' (*that which Jesus possesses*)

      b. That the Spirit would _____ (*to disclose*) it to the disciples

31. What did Jesus say would happen, after a little while (*v.16*)[92]?

_____

32. What did He say would happen, after another little while (*v.16*)?

_____

_____

[90] *John 16:12*: To bear means *to understand and receive it in a calm manner*
[91] *John 16:14*: Jesus is explaining that the Spirit would receive instruction from the Son to give to the believer
[92] *John 16:16*: To see means *to behold or look upon with the eyes*

33. Why did He say these things (*v.16*)?

_____

34. What did some of Jesus' disciples say among themselves (*v.17*)?

_____

35. What had Jesus said that confused them (*v.17*)?

      a. "A little while and you all will not _____ me…"

      b. "Again, a little while and you all will _____ me…"

      c. "Because I _____ to the Father."

36. Because Jesus said these things, what did they have to say (*v.18*)?

_____

37. What statement of Jesus' confused them (*v.18*)?

_____

38. What did they say about that statement (*v.18*)?

_____

39. What did Jesus know regarding His disciples (*v.19*)?

_____

40. What did He say to them (*v.19*)?

_____

41. What had He said that confused them (*v.19*)?

      a. "A little while and you all will not _____ me…"

      b. "Again, a little while and you all will _____ me."

42. What did Jesus then say would happen to the disciples, went He went away (*v.20*)?

      a. They would _____ (*to weep as a sign of pain or grief*)

      b. They would _____ (*to mourn*)

43. What did He say the world would do (*v.20*)?

_____

44. What did He say would happen to the disciples' sorrow (*v.20*)?

_____

45. What did Jesus say about a woman in travail (*to be in the midst of giving birth*) (*v.21*)?

_____

46. Why is this the case (*v.21*)?

_____

47. What happens to the woman, as soon as she delivers the child (**v.21**)?

_____

48. Why is this the case (**v.21**)[93]?

_____

49. Because of the trouble of Jesus' hour, what did the disciple have (**v.22**)?

_____

50. What did Jesus say would happen to them afterwards (**v.22**)?

      a. "I will _____ you again…"

      b. "Your heart will _____…"

      c. "No man will take your _____ from you."

51. What did He say would happen in that day (**v.23**)[94]?

_____

52. What did Jesus then say would happen, if they asked the Father anything in Jesus' name (**v.23**)?

_____

53. Who do we pray through to receive answers to prayer (**v.23**)?

_____

54. Had Jesus' disciples asked the Father anything in His name before this time (**v.24**)?

_____

55. What could they expect, when they asked the Father for anything in Jesus name (**v.24**)?

      a. They could _____

      b. They would _____

56. Why would this happen (**v.24**)?

_____

57. What did Jesus say that He had spoken in regarding these things (**v.25**)[95]?

_____

58. What did sort of time did He say was coming (**v.25**)?

      a. When He would not speak in _____

      b. When He would show them _____ from the Father

59. What did Jesus say would happen in that day (*at that time*) (**v.26**)?

_____

_____

[93] **John 16:21**: A man means *a human being* (male or female)
[94] **John 16:23**: To ask means *to question*
[95] **John 16:25**: A proverb is *a symbolic or figurative saying*

60. What did He say that He would not do for them (**v.26**)[96]?

_____

61. Why would He not do this for His disciples (**v.27**)?

_____

62. Why did the Father feel this way toward them (**v.27**)?

    a. Because they _____ Jesus

    b. Because they _____ that Jesus came out from (_to come_

    out from a place) God

63. What did Jesus then say about Himself (**v.28**)?

    a. "I came forth (_to be sent from Heaven_) from the _____..."

    b. "I am come into the _____..."

    c. "Again, I leave the _____..."

    d. "I go to the _____."

64. What did His disciples say in reply (**v.29**)?

    a. "Lo (_Behold_), now you speak _____..."

    b. "You do not speak a _____."

65. What else did they say about Jesus (**v.30**)?

    a. "Now we are sure that you _____ all things..."

    b. "Now we are sure that you do not need that any man should _____ (_to_

    question) you."

66. What did they say they believed, because of Jesus' sayings (**v.30**)?

_____

67. What was Jesus' question to them, in reply (**v.31**)?

_____

68. What hour (_period of time_) did Jesus tell His disciples was coming and had now come (**v.32**)?

    a. That they all would be _____ (_to be terror stricken and_

    driven in all directions)

    b. That they all would leave Him _____

69. When the disciples did this, what would happen to them (**v.32**)[97]?

_____

_____

[96] **John 16:26**: To pray the Father for you means "**To pray to the Father on your behalf**."
[97] **John 16:32**: To his own means _to his own land or native home_

70. Despite all this, what did Jesus say about His situation (*v.32*)?

_____

71. Why was this true (*v.32*)?

_____

72. Why did Jesus speak all these things to His disciples (*v.33*)[98]?

_____

73. Where does this peace come from (*v.33*)?

_____

74. What did He say the disciples would have in the world (*v.33*)[99]?

_____

75. Despite this, what did He command them to do (*v.33*)[100]?

_____

76. Why should they do this (*v.33*)[101]?

_____

77. Do you believe that we can be of good courage through Jesus today (*v.33*)?

_____

78. Do you believe that He has overcome the world, to allow all believers to have the victory through Him today (*v.33*)?

_____

_____

---

[98] *John 16:33*: Peace means *the divine tranquility that comes to those that believe in Jesus Christ for salvation and await His return to establish His Kingdom*

[99] *John 16:33*: Tribulation means *distress, affliction, and oppression*

[100] *John 16:33*: To be of good cheer means *to be of good courage*

[101] *John 16:33*: To overcome the world means *to overcome the world's ability to harm the believer and subvert the things of Christ through its influence*

Meditation (What God Spoke to Me About):

_____
_____
_____
_____
_____
_____
_____
_____

Application (How I Can Apply What I Learned):

_____
_____
_____
_____
_____
_____
_____
_____

Memorization (How I Can Retain What I Read):

Suggestions: *John 16:1-3; 16:7-11; 16:13-16; 16:22-24; 16:32-33*

_____
_____
_____

Assessment (How I Am Doing With My Application and Memorization):

_____
_____
_____
_____
_____
_____

Bible Study Questions (*John 17:1-26*)

Instructions: Pray that God will help you to understand this passage. Read through this Bible passage twice: once for reading and another time for understanding. After reading, consider and answer the questions listed below. Write down notes regarding anything else God spoke to you about.

1. After speaking to His disciples, what does John tell us that Jesus did next (*v.1*)?

_____

2. What did Jesus pray to His Father (*v.1*)?

    a. "The _____ (*a period of time*) has come."

    b. "_____ (*to make one's worth to be revealed*) your Son…"

3. Why did He want God to do this (*v.1*)?

_____

4. What did Jesus say that His Father had given Him (*v.2*)[102]?

_____

5. Why did God give Him this (*v.2*)[103]?

_____

_____

6. Why has God allowed believers to have eternal life (*v.3*)?

    a. That they might _____ the only true God

    b. That they might _____ Jesus Christ

7. Who was sent by the Father to come to Earth and preach the truth (*v.3*)?

_____

8. What did Jesus say that He did (*v.4*)?

    a. He _____ (*to make one's worth to be revealed*) God on Earth

    b. He _____ the work God gave Him to do

9. Because of these things, what did Jesus ask His Father to do (*v.5*)?

_____

10. How was He looking to be glorified (*v.5*)[104]?

_____

---

[102] **John 17:2**: Power over all flesh means *authority over mankind* (speaking of Jesus' authority over all men)

[103] **John 17:2**: To give means *to furnish* (in this case: God furnished Jesus with a certain number of believers to follow after Him and serve Him on Earth)

[104] **John 17:5**: Glory means *a most exalted state* (speaking of the glory Jesus had in Heaven, before coming to Earth)

11. When did Jesus have this sort of glory (**v.5**)[105]?

_____

12. What else did Jesus say that He did (**v.6**)[106]?

_____

13. Who was this manifested to (**v.6**)[107]?

_____

14. What did He say about these people to His Father (**v.6**)?

      a. "_____ were yours…"

      b. "You _____ them to me…"

      c. "They have _____ (*to observe*) your Word."

15. What did Jesus tell His Father that the disciples knew about Him (**v.7**)[108]?

_____

_____

16. Why did He mention this (**v.8**)?

      a. Because Jesus had _____ the disciples the words that God

      _____ to Him

      b. Because they had _____ those words

      c. Because they knew that Jesus _____ out from God

      d. Because they had believed that God _____ Jesus

17. Who did Jesus say that He prayed for (**v.9**)?

_____

18. Who did He pray for specifically (**v.9**)?

      a. Not for the _____ (*the ungodly multitude*)

      b. For them that God had _____ Him

19. Why did He pray for these people (**v.9-10**)?

      a. Because _____ are God's

      b. Because _____ that are Christ's are God's (**v.10**)

      c. Because _____ that are God's are Christ's

      d. Because Jesus is _____ in them

---

[105] **John 17:5**: Before the world was means *before the earth existed* (revealing Jesus' deity)
[106] **John 17:6**: To manifest means *to reveal*
[107] **John 17:6**: Out of the world means *out of the ungodly multitude*
[108] **John 17:7** (lit.): "**Now they have known that everything you have given me is from you.**"

20. What did Jesus say about His current situation (*v.11*)[109]?

_____

21. What did He say about His disciples' situation (*v.11*)?

_____

22. What did He say that He was in the process of doing (*v.11*)?

_____

23. How did Jesus address God (*v.11*)[110]?

_____

24. What did He ask God to do for Him (*v.11*)[111]?

_____

25. Why did He ask Him to do this (*v.11*)[112]?

_____

26. How can we persevere and stand for the truth in this world (*v.11*)?

_____

27. What did Jesus say that He did, while He was with the disciples in the world (*v.12*)[113]?

_____

28. What else did He say about those that God gave Him (*v.12*)?

    a. That He _____ (*to guard*) them

    b. That none of them were _____ (*to be destroyed*)

29. Who was the only disciple that was lost (*v.12*)[114]?

_____

30. Why did this have to happen (*v.12*)?

_____

31. As Jesus continued to speak with His Father, what did He say that He did (*v.13*)?

    a. "Now I _____ to You…"

    b. "These things I _____ in the world…"

_____

[109] *John 17:11*: To be in the world means *to be in the world to dwell among men*
[110] *John 17:11*: Holy means *perfect, pure, and sinless*
[111] *John 17:11*: To keep means *to cause one to persevere of stand firm*
[112] *John 17:11*: To be one means *to be unified in desire, instead of divided*
[113] *John 17:12*: To keep means *to guard from outside assaults*
[114] *John 17:12*: Perdition means *destruction and eternal misery*

32. Why did He speak these things (*v.13*)[115]?

_____

33. What did Jesus say that He gave to His disciples (*v.14*)?

_____

34. What was the result of this (*v.14*)?

_____

35. Why did this happen (*v.14*)[116]?

_____

36. Why was this the case with Jesus' disciples (*v.14*)?

_____

37. What else did Jesus pray to God for His disciples (*v.15*)[117]?

     a. Not that He would take them out of the _____

     b. That He would _____ them from the evil

38. What else did Jesus say about His disciples (*v.16*)[118]?

_____

39. What did He say about Himself (*v.16*)?

_____

40. What else did Jesus ask His Father to do for His disciples (*v.17*)[119]?

_____

41. Through what medium does this happen (*v.17*)?

_____

42. What is truth (*absolute truth*) (*v.17*)?

_____

43. What had the Father done to the Son (*v.18*)?

_____

44. What had the Son done to His disciples (*v.18*)?

_____

_____

[115] *John 17:13*: To fulfill means *to make complete in every respect* (in this case: the joy Jesus provides to believers)
[116] *John 17:14*: To not be of the world means *to not be a part of the ungodly multitude* (in both cases)
[117] *John 17:15*: To keep them from the evil means *to guard the disciples from Satan's assaults*
[118] *John 17:16*: To not be of the world means *to not be a part of the ungodly multitude* (in both cases)
[119] *John 17:17*: To sanctify means *to purify internally*

45. What did Jesus do for the sakes of His disciples (*v.19*)[120]?

_____

46. Why did He do this (*v.19*)[121]?

_____

47. How are we sanctified (*v.19*)?

_____

48. Who else did Jesus pray to God for (*v.20*)?

    a. Not for His disciples _____

    b. For them which should _____ on Jesus through the word of

    the disciples

49. Have you believed on Jesus Christ as for salvation through God's Word?

_____

50. Do you believe that Jesus is speaking about you in this verse (*v.20*)?

_____

51. Why did He pray for these people too (*v.21*)[122]?

_____

52. Why did He pray for this (*v.21*)?

    a. That they might be _____ in the Father and Son

    b. That the world might _____ that the Father sent the Son

53. What special relationship do God the Father and Son have (*v.21*)?

    a. The _____ is one in the Son (*Jesus Christ*)

    b. The _____ is one in the Father

54. What did Jesus say that He had given to those that the Father gave Him (*v.22*)?

_____

55. Why did He do this (*v.22*)[123]?

_____

56. Are God the Father and Son united or divided (*v.22*)?

_____

_____

[120] **John 17:19**: To sanctify means *to consecrate oneself toward holy things*
[121] **John 17:19**: To be sanctified means *to be purified internally*
[122] **John 17:21**: To be one means *to be unified in desire, instead of divided*
[123] **John 17:22**: To be one means *to be unified in desire, instead of divided*

57. If they are like this, should all that believe in Jesus, based upon the truth of God's Word, be united or divided (*v.22*)?

_____

58. How were God the Son, God the Father, and the disciples of Christ united as one (*v.23*)?

       a. _____ is in the disciples

       b. The _____ is in Jesus Christ

59. Why did Jesus desire this for all that believed in Him (*v.23*)?

       a. So that His disciples could be made _____ (*to be perfectly united*) in one

       b. So that the _____ would know that the Father sent Jesus

       c. So that the _____ would know that the Father loved them

60. How much does God the Father love the world (*the ungodly multitude*) (*v.23*)?

_____

61. What did Jesus also desire for those that the Father had given Him (*v.24*)?

_____

62. Why did He want this to occur (*v.24*)?

_____

63. Who had given this to Jesus (*v.24*)?

_____

64. Why had He done this (*v.24*)?

_____

_____

65. What title did Jesus next use for the Father (*v.25*)[124]?

_____

66. What did Jesus say about the world (*v.25*)?

_____

67. What did He say about Himself (*v.25*)?

_____

---

[124] *John 17:25*: Righteous speaks of *God being the just judge; rendering a different fate to those that believe in Jesus Christ than those that reject Him*

68. What did He say about His disciples (*v.25-26*)?

      a. That they _____ that the Father had sent Jesus Christ

      b. That Jesus _____ the Father's name to them

69. What did Jesus say that He would continue to do (*v.26*)?

_____

70. Why did He say that He would do this (*v.27*)?

      a. That the _____ that the Father _____ Him with would

      be in the disciples

      b. That Jesus Christ would be _____ His disciples

Meditation (What God Spoke to Me About):

_____
_____
_____
_____
_____
_____
_____
_____

Application (How I Can Apply What I Learned):

_____
_____
_____
_____
_____
_____
_____
_____
_____

Memorization (How I Can Retain What I Read):

Suggestions: *John 17:11-12; 17:14-17; 17:20-21; 17:25-26*

_____
_____
_____
_____

Assessment (How I Am Doing With My Application and Memorization):

_____
_____
_____
_____
_____
_____
_____

Bible Study Questions (*John 18:1-40*)

Instructions: Pray that God will help you to understand this passage. Read through this Bible passage twice: once for reading and another time for understanding. After reading, consider and answer the questions listed below. Write down notes regarding anything else God spoke to you about.

1. After giving the Upper Room Discourse (*John 14-17*), what did Jesus and His disciples do next (*v.1*)[125]?

_____

2. What was at the place they travelled to (*v.1*)?

_____

3. What did Jesus and His disciples do, when they got there (*v.1*)?

_____

4. Who also knew about this place (*v.2*)?

_____

5. What would this man do to Jesus (*v.2*)?

_____

6. Why did this man know about this place (*v.2*)[126]?

_____

7. What had Judas received (*v.3*)?

    a. A band (*a company of soldiers*) of _____

    b. A band of _____ (*the servants or officers of the Sanhedrin*)

8. Who did he receive these men from (*v.3*)?

    a. The chief _____

    b. The _____

9. What did these people come to the garden with (*v.3*)?

    a. _____ (*torches*)

    b. _____ (*oil-fed lamps*)

    c. _____

10. Because of these things, what did Jesus know (*v.4*)?

_____

11. What did He do (*v.4*)?

_____

---

[125] *John 18:1*: Brook means *a torrent of water that flowed in winter*
[126] *John 18:2*: To resort means *to gather together*

12. What did He say to the crowd (**v.4**)?

_____

13. What was their answer (**v.5**)?

_____

14. What did Jesus say to them (**v.5**)?

_____

15. Who stood with the crowd of men that sought Jesus (**v.5**)?

_____

16. What happened, as soon as Jesus answered the crowd's question (**v.6**)?

       a. They went _____

       b. They _____ to the ground

17. What did Jesus ask them a second time (**v.7**)?

_____

18. What did they answer (**v.7**)?

_____

19. What did Jesus then say to the crowd (**v.8**)?

_____

20. If they sought Him, what did Jesus tell them to do with His disciples (**v.8**)?

_____

21. Why did He say this (**v.9**)?

_____

22. What saying had He spoken (**v.9**)[127]?

_____

23. Which of the disciples had a sword with him (**v.10**)?

_____

24. What did he do with it (**v.10**)?

       a. He _____ (*to unsheathe*) it

       b. He _____ (*to strike*) the high priest's servant

       c. He cut off his right _____

_____

[127] **John 18:9**: To be lost means *to be spiritually destroyed*

25. What was the servant's name (**v.10**)[128]?

_____

26. What did Jesus order Peter to do (**v.11**)?

_____

27. What did He say about the cup that His Father had given Him (**v.11**)[129]?

_____

28. What did the crowd do to Jesus (**v.12-13**)[130]?

   a. They _____ (*to seize one as a prisoner*) Him

   b. They _____ (*to fasten with chains*) Him

   c. They _____ Him away (**v.13**)

29. Who did they bring Jesus to first (**v.13**)[131]?

_____

30. Who was this man the father-in-law of (**v.13**)[132]?

_____

31. What was Caiaphas' position (**v.13**)[133]?

_____

32. What had this man previously done (**v.14**)?

_____

33. What had he said to them (**v.14**)[134]?

_____

34. Who followed Jesus (**v.15**)?

   a. Simon _____

   b. Another _____

_____

[128] *John 18:10*: Malchus means *king or kingdom*
[129] *John 18:11*: The cup is figurative of the divine appointment of God, whether favorable or unfavorable, that God presents to one to drink in life
[130] *John 18:12*: Captain means *the commander of a Roman military tribune*
[131] *John 18:13*: Annas was a former high priest that had great influence among the Jews
[132] *John 18:13*: Caiaphas was the high priest of the Temple in Jesus' day
[133] *John 18:13*: The duties of the high priest in Jesus' day included performing the common duties of a priest, entering the holy of holies to offer atonement for the people and himself (which was a unique duty), and to preside over the Sanhedrin (or supreme Council), when convened for judicial deliberations
[134] *John 18:14*: Expedient means *profitable*

35. What was special about this other disciple (**v.15**)?

    a. He was _____ to the high priest

    b. He went in with _____ into the palace (*house*) of the high priest

36. What did Peter do (**v.16**)[135]?

_____

37. What did the other disciple do (**v.16**)?

    a. He went _____

    b. He _____ to her that kept the door (*the doorkeeper*)

    c. He brought in _____

38. Who asked Peter a question (**v.17**)[136]?

_____

39. What did she ask Peter (**v.17**)?

_____

40. What was his answer (**v.17**)?

_____

41. Who else stood there (**v.18**)?

    a. The _____

    b. The _____ (*officers of the Sanhedrin*)

42. What had they done there (**v.18**)?

_____

43. Why had they done this (**v.18**)?

_____

44. What did they do at this place (**v.18**)?

_____

45. What did Peter do there (**v.18**)?

    a. He _____ with them

    b. He _____ himself

46. Who began to ask Jesus questions (**v.19**)?

_____

_____

[135] **John 18:16**: Without means *out of doors* (outside)
[136] **John 18:17**: A damsel is *a maidservant*

47. What did he ask Him (**v.19**)?

      a. About His _____ (*learners*)

      b. About His _____ (*beliefs and teachings*)

48. What was Jesus' answer (**v.20**)?

_____

49. Where did He say that He taught (**v.20**)?

      a. In the _____ (*the Jews' place of assembly to follow Judaism*)

      b. In the _____ (*the Jews' chief place of worship*)

50. What happened at these two places (**v.20**)[137]?

_____

51. What did Jesus say that He had said in secret (**v.20**)?

_____

52. What did He ask the high priest (**v.21**)?

_____

53. What did He tell him to do (**v.21**)?

_____

54. Why did He tell him to do this (**v.21**)?

_____

55. What happened, after Jesus said these words (**v.22**)[138]?

_____

56. What did he strike him with (**v.22**)?

_____

57. What did he say to Jesus (**v.22**)?

_____

58. What was Jesus' response (**v.23**)?

      a. "If I have spoken _____, bear witness of the _____..."

      b. "If I have spoken _____, why do you smite (*to beat*) me?"

59. Who sent Jesus bound (*to fasten with chains*) to the high priest (**v.24**)?

_____

---

[137] **John 18:20**: To resort means *to gather together*
[138] **John 18:22**: To strike means *to slap in the face*

60. What was the high priest's name (*v.24*)?

_____

61. What did Simon Peter do (*v.25*)?

        a. He _____

        b. He _____ himself

62. Because of this, what did the people standing around the fire ask him (*v.25*)?

_____

63. Did Peter confirm this or deny it (*v.25*)?

_____

64. What did he say to them (*v.25*)?

_____

65. Who was one of the men standing around the fire (*v.26*)?

        a. One of the _____ of the high priest

        b. A _____ (*one related by blood*) of the man whose ear Peter had

        cut off

66. What did this man ask Peter (*v.26*)?

_____

67. Did Peter confirm or deny this (*v.27*)?

_____

68. What happened immediately after Peter said these things (*v.27*)[139]?

_____

69. Where did they lead Jesus to from Caiaphas' house (*v.28*)[140]?

_____

70. What time of day was it (*v.28*)?

_____

71. Did the Jews enter into the judgment hall (*v.28*)?

_____

---

[139] *John 18:27*: A cock is *a rooster*
[140] *John 18:28*: The hall of judgment was *the palace where the governor of a province resided* (in this case: Pilate)

72. Why did they do this (***v.28***)[141]?

      a. Lest they would be _____ (*to be defiled in a ritual sense*)

      b. So that they might eat the _____

73. Who went out to speak with the people (***v.29***)[142]?

_____

74. What did he ask the Jews (***v.29***)?

_____

75. What was their answer to him (***v.30***)[143]?

_____

_____

76. What did Pilate say in response (***v.31***)?

      a. "You all _____ Him…"

      b. "You all _____ Him according to your law."

77. What did the Jews say in response (***v.31***)?

_____

78. Why did they say this (***v.32***)?

_____

79. What was the prophecy Jesus had spoken (***v.32***)?

_____

80. What did Pilate do then (***v.33***)?

      a. He _____ into the judgment hall

      b. He _____ Jesus

81. What did he ask Jesus (***v.33***)?

_____

82. What was Jesus' response (***v.34***)?

      a. "Do you _____ this thing of yourself?"

      b. "Did others _____ it to you about me?"

---

[141] ***John 18:28***: The Passover is observed on the fourteenth day of Nisan (the Jews' first month of the year) in order to commemorate the day their fathers departed from Egypt. By God's decree, they were to slay and eat a lamb and to sprinkle its blood upon the doorposts of their homes, so that the death angel would pass by

[142] ***John 18:29***: Pilate was the Roman governor of Judaea and Samaria during the time of Jesus' death

[143] ***John 18:30***: A malefactor is *an evil-doer*

83. What did Pilate ask Him in reply (**v.35**)?

_____

84. What did he say had happened to Jesus (**v.35**)?

      a. "Your own _____ (*a people group*) has delivered you to me…"

      b. "Your own chief _____ have delivered you to me."

85. What else did he ask Jesus (**v.35**)?

_____

86. What was Jesus' answer (**v.36**)?

_____

87. What did He say would happen, if His kingdom was of this world (**v.36**)?

_____

88. Why would they do this (**v.36**)?

_____

89. Where did He say that His kingdom was (**v.36**)?

_____

90. What was Pilate's question to Jesus' statements (**v.37**)?

_____

91. What did Jesus reply (**v.37**)?

_____

92. Why did Jesus say that He was born as a man (**v.37**)[144]?

_____

93. For what cause was Jesus born into the world (**v.37**)?

_____

94. What did He say about those that were of the truth (**v.37**)?

_____

95. What was Pilate's response (**v.38**)?

_____

96. After saying this, what did he do (**v.38**)?

_____

97. What did he say to them (**v.38**)?

_____

_____

[144] **John 18:37**: To this end means *for this reason*

98. What did he say that the Jews had (**v.39**)[145]?

_____

99. What was this practice (**v.39**)[146]?

_____

100. Because of this practice, what did he ask them (**v.39**)?

_____

_____

101. What did the Jews cry out in reply (**v.40**)?

_____

102. Who was this man (**v.40**)[147]?

_____

---

[145] **John 18:39**: Custom means _a habitual practice_
[146] **John 18:39**: To release means _to release a prisoner_
[147] **John 18:40**: Robber means _a plunderer or brigand_ (one that robs by force)

Meditation (What God Spoke to Me About):

_____
_____
_____
_____
_____
_____
_____
_____

Application (How I Can Apply What I Learned):

_____
_____
_____
_____
_____
_____
_____
_____

Memorization (How I Can Retain What I Read):

Suggestions: *John 18:4-9; 18:36-38*

_____
_____
_____

Assessment (How I Am Doing With My Application and Memorization):

_____
_____
_____
_____
_____
_____

Bible Study Questions (*John 19:1-42*)

Instructions: Pray that God will help you to understand this passage. Read through this Bible passage twice: once for reading and another time for understanding. After reading, consider and answer the questions listed below. Write down notes regarding anything else God spoke to you about.

1. Because of the Jews' decision, what did Pilate do with Jesus (*v.1*)[148]?

    a. He _____ Him

    b. He _____ Him

2. What did the soldiers do to Jesus (*v.2*)[149]?

    a. They _____ (*to weave together*) a crown of thorns

    b. They put it upon His _____

    c. They put on Him a purple _____ (*a cloak*)

3. What did the soldiers say to Jesus (*v.3*)[150]?

_____

4. What did they do, after they said this (*v.3*)?

_____

5. After doing these things, what did Pilate do again (*v.4*)[151]?

_____

6. What did he say to the Jews (*v.4*)?

_____

7. Why did he do this (*v.4*)[152]?

_____

8. Who did he bring forth (*v.5*)?

_____

9. What was He wearing (*v.5*)?

    a. The _____ of thorns

    b. The _____ robe

10. What did Pilate say about Him (*v.5*)?

_____
_____

---

[148] *John 19:1*: To scourge means *to take a cat of nine tails (a whip with five to nine lashes) and beat the victim with it thirty-nine times* (oftentimes the victim did not survive the scourging)
[149] *John 19:2*: The soldiers were common Roman soldiers
[150] *John 19:3*: Hail was *a greeting given as a wish for that person to thrive*
[151] *John 19:3*: To smite means *to strike*
[152] *John 19:4*: Fault means *a cause for which to punish a person*

11. Who saw Jesus, after Pilate brought Him forth (**v.6**)?

      a. The chief _____

      b. The _____ (*the servants of the Sanhedrin*)

12. What did they cry out twice (**v.6**)[153]?

_____

13. What was Pilate's response (**v.6**)?

      a. "You all _____ Him…"

      b. "You all _____ Him."

14. Why did he say this (**v.6**)?

_____

15. How did the Jews answer him (**v.7**)?

      a. "We have a _____…"

      b. "By our _____ He ought to die…"

16. Why did they say that Jesus deserved to die (**v.7**)?

_____

17. What happened to Pilate, when he heard that saying (**v.8**)?

_____

18. Because of this, what did he do (**v.9**)?

_____

19. What did he say to Jesus (**v.9**)[154]?

_____

20. What was Jesus' answer (**v.9**)?

_____

21. How did Pilate react to this (**v.10**)?

      a. "Do you not _____ to me?"

      b. "Do you not know that I have the power to _____ you?"

      c. "Do you not know that I have the power to _____ (*to release a captive and set him free*) you?"

---

[153] **John 19:6**: To crucify a person means *to nail a person to a cross for the purpose of torturing and suffocating the victim to death*

[154] **John 19:9**: Whence art thou means "***Where are you from?***"

22. What did Jesus say to this (**v.11**)[155]?

_____

_____

23. Because of this, who did He say did the greater sin (**v.11**)[156]?

_____

24. What did Pilate seek to do from that time forward (**v.12**)?

_____

25. What did the Jews cry out in opposition to Pilate's desires (**v.12**)[157]?

_____

26. What did they say about those that make themselves to be kings (**v.12**)?

_____

27. What did Pilate do, when he heard the Jews' sayings (**v.13**)?

    a. He _____ Jesus forth

    b. He sat down in the _____ seat (*the official seat of a judge*)

28. What was the name of this place (**v.13**)[158]?

_____

29. What was its name in Hebrew (**v.13**)[159]?

_____

30. During what time of day did these things occur (**v.14**)[160]?

    a. During the _____ of the Passover

    b. About the _____ hour (*about noontime*)

31. What did Pilate declare to the Jews (**v.14**)?

_____

32. What did the Jews cry out, when they saw Jesus (**v.15**)?

    a. "_____ with Him!"

    b. "_____ with Him!"

    c. "_____ Him!"

---

[155] **John 19:11**: From above means *from Heaven* (specifically: God's throne)
[156] **John 19:11**: To be delivered means *to deliver one up to judgment, sentencing, and death*
[157] **John 19:12**: Friend means *one that is loyal to another's interests* (in this case: Caesar's)
[158] **John 19:13**: The Pavement was a place paved with a mosaic and was near the palace at Jerusalem
[159] **John 19:13**: Gabbatha means *a raised or elevated place*
[160] **John 19:14**: The preparation of the Passover means *they prepared for the next day's Sabbath on the Passover*

33. What did Pilate ask the crowd (*v.15*)?

_____

34. What was the answer of the chief priests (*v.15*)?

_____

35. Because of this, what did Pilate do to Jesus (*v.16*)?

_____

36. What did the soldiers do to Jesus (*v.16*)?

      a. They _____ Him

      b. The _____ Him away

37. What did they make Jesus do (*v.17*)?

      a. He bore (*to carry*) His _____

      b. He went forth to a place called the place of a _____

38. What was the name of this place in Hebrew (*v.17*)[161]?

_____

39. What did they do to Jesus in that place (*v.18*)?

_____

40. How many others had the same fate as Jesus (*v.18*)?

_____

41. How were they all positioned (*v.18*)?

      a. Each one on either _____

      b. Jesus in the _____ (*the middle*)

42. What did Pilate then do (*v.19*)?

      a. He _____ a title (an inscription that gave the accusation or crime for which a criminal suffered)

      b. He put it on the _____

43. What did the inscription say (*v.19*)?

_____

44. Who read this title (*v.20*)?

_____

_____

[161] *John 19:17*: Golgotha means *a skull*

45. Why did this happen (**v.20**)[162]?

_____

_____

46. In what languages was this title written (**v.20**)?

_____

47. What did the chief priests say to Pilate (**v.21**)?

      a. "Write not, "The _____ of the Jews…'"

      b. "Write that He said, 'I am _____ of the Jews.'"

48. What was Pilate's reply to them (**v.22**)?

_____

49. What did the soldiers do, after they had crucified Jesus (**v.23**)?

      a. They took His _____

      b. They made _____ parts

50. Why did they make this many parts out of Jesus' garments (**v.23**)?

_____

51. What other piece of clothing did they take (**v.23**)[163]?

_____

52. What was special about this piece of clothing (**v.23**)?

      a. It was without a _____

      b. It was _____ from the top throughout

53. Because of this, what did the soldiers say about it (**v.24**)?

      a. "Let us not _____ (_to divide by tearing_) it…"

      b. "Let us _____ lots (_a form of gambling_) for it, whose it will be."

54. Why did this happen (**v.24**)?

_____

55. What did this scripture say (**v.24**)?

      a. "They _____ my raiment among them…"

      b. "For my _____ (_tunic_), they did cast lots."

56. Did the Roman soldiers act according to this prophecy (**v.24**)?

_____

---

[162] **John 19:20**: Nigh means _close_

[163] **John 19:23**: Jesus' coat was _a tunic or undergarment worn next to the skin_

57. Who stood by the cross of Jesus (**v.25**)[164] [165] [166]?

        a. Jesus' _____ (*Mary*)

        b. Jesus' mother's sister, _____ the wife of Cleophas

        c. _____ Magdalene

58. Who did Jesus see standing by the cross (**v.26**)?

        a. His _____

        b. The _____ whom He loved

59. What did He say to His mother (**v.26**)?

_____

60. What did He say to the disciple (*John*) (**v.27**)[167]?

_____

61. What did that disciple do, from that hour (*a period of time*) (**v.27**)?

_____

62. After saying this, what did Jesus know (**v.28**)?

_____

63. Because of this, what did He say (**v.28**)?

_____

64. Why did He say this (**v.28**)[168]?

_____

65. What was set in that place (**v.29**)[169]?

_____

66. What did they do with this for Jesus (**v.29**)?

        a. They filled a _____ (*a sponge*) with the vinegar

        b. They put it upon _____ (*a plant with a woody stalk*)

        c. They put it to His _____

---

[164] **John 19:25**: Jesus' aunt, Mary (cf. **Mark 15:40**) was married to Cleophas and had a son (James the less); it is deduced that Cleophas was also called Alphaeus (cf. **Matthew 10:3**)

[165] **John 19:25**: Mary Magdalene was a woman from Magdala, a town on the western coast of the Sea of Galilee, that followed Jesus

[166] **John 19:25**: Jesus not only had male disciples, but female ones as well. These godly ladies helped provide for the needs of Jesus' ministry (cf. **Mark 15:40-41**)

[167] **John 19:27**: We can find in other Gospel records that John was standing by the cross with his mother, Salome, who also heard Jesus' command to take care of His mother, Mary (cf. **Mark 15:40-41**)

[168] **John 19:28**: cf. **Psalm 69:21**

[169] **John 19:29**: This vinegar was *a mixture of sour wine and water, which the Romans soldiers were used to drinking*

67. What did Jesus say, after He had received (*to drink*) the vinegar (**v.30**)[170]?

_____

68. After He said this, what did He do (**v.30**)?

    a. He _____ His head

    b. He gave up (*to deliver up*) the _____ (*the spirit of a man*)

69. Around the time of Jesus' death, what did the Jews do (**v.31**)[171]?

_____

70. What did they request of Pilate (**v.31**)?

    a. That the _____ of those on the crosses be broken

    b. That those on the crosses be _____ away (*to be removed*)

71. Why did they ask this (**v.31**)[172]?

    a. Because it was the _____ (*the day on which the Jews made preparation to celebrate the Sabbath or a feast*)

    b. So that the bodies would not remain on the crosses for the _____ day

72. Why did they not want the bodies on the crosses for this day (**v.31**)[173]?

_____

73. What did the Roman soldiers do as a result (**v.32**)?

    a. They _____

    b. They _____ the legs of the first and other men that were crucified with Jesus

74. What did the soldiers see, when they came to Jesus (**v.33**)?

_____

75. Did they break His legs (**v.33**)?

_____

76. What did one of the soldiers do instead (**v.34**)?

_____

77. What did he use to do this (**v.34**)?

_____

---

[170] **John 19:30**: It is finished means "**Everything has been accomplished that I have been given to do by the Father**."

[171] **John 19:31**: Besought means *to request*

[172] **John 19:31**: The preparation refers to the Jews' preparing to observe the Sabbath day, which included preparing two days' worth of food (for the Sabbath and the day after), since they could not work on the Sabbath

[173] **John 19:31**: A high day means *a day above other days* (in this case it was the Sabbath)

78. What happened, when the soldier did this (*v.34*)?

_____

79. What did the man that saw these things (*the apostle John*) do (*v.35*)[174]?

_____

80. What is special about his record (*witness*) (*v.35*)?

_____

81. What did John know about what he said in his letter (*v.35*)?

_____

82. Why did he write these things (*v.35*)?

_____

83. Why did the Roman soldiers do these things to Jesus (*v.36*)?

_____

84. What did the scripture say about this event (*v.36*)[175]?

_____

85. What did another scripture say about this event (*v.37*)[176]?

_____

86. After this, who came to Pilate (*v.38*)[177]?

_____

87. What relationship did this man have with Jesus (*v.38*)[178]?

_____

88. Was he a public or secret disciple (*v.38*)?

_____

89. Why was this the case (*v.38*)?

_____

90. What did he ask Pilate for (*v.38*)?

_____

91. What was Pilate's response (*v.38*)[179]?

_____

---

[174] *John 19:35*: To bear record means *to bear witness of a thing*
[175] *John 19:36*: cf. *Exodus 12:46; Numbers 9:12; 1 Corinthians 5:7*
[176] *John 19:37*: cf. *Zechariah 12:10; Revelation 1:7*
[177] *John 19:38*: Arimathaea was a town in Israel; probably located near Mount Ephraim where Samuel was born
[178] *John 19:38*: Disciple means *a learner or pupil*
[179] *John 19:38*: To give leave means *to give permission to a person*

92. Because of this, what did Joseph do (**v.38**)?

     a. He _____

     b. He _____ the body of Jesus

93. Who also came with Joseph (**v.39**)[180]?

_____

94. What had this man done at the first (*to begin with*) (**v.39**)?

_____

95. What did he bring with him (**v.39**)[181] [182]?

_____

96. How much of this did he bring with him (**v.39**)[183]?

_____

97. What did these men do with the body of Jesus (**v.40**)?

     a. They _____ it

     b. They _____ it in linen clothes (*strips of linen cloth*), with the spices

98. Why did they do this (**v.40**)?

_____

99. What was in the place where Jesus was crucified (**v.41**)?

_____

100. What was in this place (**v.41**)[184]?

_____

101. What was special about it (**v.41**)?

_____

102. Why did they lay Jesus there (**v.42**)[185]?

     a. Because of the Jews' _____ day

     b. Because the _____ (*tomb*) was nigh (*close*) at hand

---

[180] **John 19:39**: Nicodemus was a Pharisee that believed in Jesus and had come to Him by night (cf. **John 3**)

[181] **John 19:39**: Myrrh was *a costly perfume used as an antiseptic for embalming in Jesus' day*

[182] **John 19:39**: Aloe was used for fumigation and embalming in Jesus' day

[183] **John 19:39**: This was about seventy-five United States pounds (those mentioned here are twelve ounce pounds)

[184] **John 19:41**: Sepulchre means *a tomb*

[185] **John 19:42**: Joseph and Nicodemus had between 3pm and 6pm to take the body of Jesus, due to the Sabbath.

Meditation (What God Spoke to Me About):

_____

_____

_____

_____

_____

_____

_____

Application (How I Can Apply What I Learned):

_____

_____

_____

_____

_____

_____

_____

_____

Memorization (How I Can Retain What I Read):

Suggestions: *John 19:1-5; 19:7-12; 19:16-19; 19:25-30*

_____

_____

_____

Assessment (How I Am Doing With My Application and Memorization):

_____

_____

_____

_____

_____

_____

Bible Study Questions (*John 20:1-31*)

Instructions: Pray that God will help you to understand this passage. Read through this Bible passage twice: once for reading and another time for understanding. After reading, consider and answer the questions listed below. Write down notes regarding anything else God spoke to you about.

1. Who came to Jesus' sepulcher (*tomb*), on the first day of the week (*Sunday*) (*v.1*)[186]?

_____

2. At what time of day did she come (*v.1*)[187]?

_____

3. When she came, what did she see (*v.1*)[188]?

_____

4. When she saw this, what did she do (*v.2*)?

    a. She _____

    b. She _____ to Peter and the other disciple (*the apostle John*), whom Jesus loved

5. What did she say to them (*v.2*)?

    a. "They have _____ away the Lord out of the sepulcher (*tomb*)…"

    b. "We do not know where they have _____ Him."

6. Because of these words, what did Peter and John do (*v.3*)?

    a. They _____ forth

    b. They _____ to the sepulcher (*tomb*)

7. How did Peter and John run (*v.4*)?

_____

8. Who outran the other; coming first to the tomb (*v.4*)?

_____

9. What did John do, when he came to the tomb (*v.5*)?

    a. He _____ down

    b. He _____ in

10. What did he see (*v.5*)[189]?

_____

_____

[186] *John 20:1*: Mary Magdalene was a woman from Magdala, a town on the western coast of the Sea of Galilee, that followed Jesus
[187] *John 20:1*: This time of day was *sometime before 6am*
[188] *John 20:1*: Joseph of Arimathaea had rolled a large stone across the entranceway of the tomb and Pilate had it sealed, while assigning a watch of Roman guards to it (cf. *Matthew 27:59-66*)
[189] *John 20:5*: The linen clothes were *strips of linen cloth used for swathing the dead*

11. Did John go into the tomb (**v.5**)?

_____

12. Who came to the tomb after John (**v.6**)?

_____

13. What did he do (**v.6-7**)[190]?

     a. He _____ the sepulcher

     b. He _____ the linen clothes lying

     c. He saw the _____ lying (**v.7**)

14. How was the napkin lying (**v.7**)?

     a. Not with the linen _____

     b. It was _____ together (*to roll up*) in a place by itself

15. After Peter went in, who else followed (**v.8**)?

_____

16. What did he do (**v.8**)?

     a. He _____

     b. He _____ (*to believe that Jesus was raised from the dead,*

     thereby making Him to be God's Son and the Messiah)

17. What did Peter and John not yet know (**v.9**)?

_____

18. What did this scripture say (**v.9**)?

_____

19. What did the disciples then do (**v.10**)[191]?

_____

20. Who stayed at the tomb (**v.11**)?

_____

21. What did she do there (**v.11**)?

_____

22. What else did she do, as she did this (**v.11**)?

     a. She _____ down

     b. She _____ into the sepulcher

_____

[190] **John 20:7**: The napkin was *a handkerchief used to swath the head of the dead*
[191] **John 20:10**: Peter and John both lived in Galilee, a province north of Jerusalem (cf. **Matthew 4:12-22**), but apparently had homes in Judaea as well (the distance between the two was about sixty-three miles)

23. What did she see (*v.12*)?

_____

24. What were they dressed in (*v.12*)[192]?

_____

25. Where were they sitting (*v.12*)?

      a. One was at the _____

      b. The other was at the _____

26. Where did they sit (*v.12*)?

_____

27. What did they ask Mary (*v.13*)?

_____

28. What was her answer (*v.13*)[193]?

      a. "Because they have _____ away my Lord…"

      b. "Because I do not know where they have _____ Him."

29. After she said this, what did she do (*v.14*)?

      a. She _____ back

      b. She saw _____ standing (*to stand in a place*)

30. Did she know that it was Jesus that she saw (*v.14*)?

_____

31. What did Jesus ask Mary Magdalene (*v.15*)?

      a. "Woman, why do you _____?"

      b. "Woman, whom do you _____?"

32. Who did Mary think that Jesus was (*v.15*)[194]?

_____

33. What did she say to Him (*v.15*)?

      a. "Sir, if you have borne (*to take away through theft*) Him from here, tell me where you have

      _____ Him…"

      b. "I will _____ (*to carry one off*) Him away."

_____

[192] **John 20:12**: White clothing means *clothing that was brilliant, shining, and dazzling from whiteness*

[193] **John 20:13**: Mary Magdalene was not a woman easily startled by spirits, as Jesus had cast many demons out of her (cf. **Mark 16:9**)

[194] **John 20:15**: Gardener means *the keeper of a garden*

34. What was Jesus' answer to her (*v.16*)?

_____

35. What did Mary do, when she heard Him (*v.16*)?

_____

36. What did she say to Him (*v.16*)[195]?

_____

37. What does this word mean (*v.16*)?

_____

38. What did Jesus say to her (*v.17*)[196]?

_____

39. Why did He say this (*v.17*)[197]?

_____

40. Instead of inspecting whether or not He was real, what did Jesus tell Mary to do (*v.17*)[198]?

_____

41. What message from Jesus was she to give to them (*v.17*)?

    a. "I _____ unto my Father…"

    b. "I _____ unto your Father…"

42. Whose God did Jesus say that His Father was (*v.17*)?

_____

43. What did Mary Magdalene do (*v.18*)?

    a. She _____

    b. She _____ the disciples that she had seen the Lord

    c. She _____ the disciples that the Lord had spoken these things to her

44. What happened that same day (*v.19*)?

    a. Jesus _____

    b. Jesus _____ in the midst (*among them*)

45. What time of day did this happen (*v.19*)[199]?

_____

---

[195] **John 20:16**: Rabboni means *Master or Chief* and was a title of honor and reverence for Jesus

[196] **John 20:17**: "Touch me not" literally means "***Do not handle me to see whether I am still clothed with a body; there is no need of such an examination.***"

[197] **John 20:17**: To ascend means *to move to a higher place* (in this case: To His Father in Heaven)

[198] **John 20:17**: Brethren means *brothers in Christ* and speaks of the apostles

[199] **John 20:19**: Evening means *from 6pm to the beginning of night*

46. During what day did this happen (*v.19*)?

_____

47. What was significant about the doors where the disciples were assembled (*v.19*)[200]?

_____

48. Why were they in this state (*v.19*)?

_____

49. When Jesus came, what did He say to the disciples (*v.19*)?

_____

50. What did He do, when He had said this (*v.20*)?

      a. He showed them His _____

      b. He showed them His _____

51. What happened to the disciples, when they saw the Lord (*v.20*)[201]?

_____

52. What did Jesus say to them again (*v.21*)?

_____

53. What did He say that His Father had done (*v.21*)?

_____

54. Because of this, what did Jesus do (*v.21*)?

_____

55. What did He do, after He said this to the disciples (*v.22*)[202]?

_____

56. What did He say to them (*v.22*)[203]?

_____

57. What did Jesus say to His disciples about those whose sins they remitted (*v.23*)[204]?

_____

---

[200] *John 20:19*: To be shut means *to be shut in order to forbid entrance to another*
[201] *John 20:20*: To be glad means *to rejoice*
[202] *John 20:22*: To breathe means *to blow*
[203] *John 20:22*: This was a symbolic act to express the communication of the Spirit of God to the disciples and the importance of the new creation that was available, because of Jesus' death, burial, and resurrection; the disciples did not receive the Spirit of God at this time (cf. *Acts 2; Ezekiel 37:5; Genesis 2:7*)
[204] *John 20:23*: To remit means *to let go of or forgive a debt, by not requiring it to be paid*

58. What did He say about those whose sins they retained (**v.23**)[205] [206]?

_____

59. Who was not there, when Jesus came (**v.24**)?

_____

60. What position did he hold (**v.24**)?

_____

61. What was he also called (**v.24**)[207]?

_____

62. Because he was not there, what did the other disciples say to him (**v.25**)?

_____

63. What did this disciple say that he would not do (**v.25**)?

_____

64. When did he say that he would believe that Jesus was alive (**v.25**)?

    a. When he saw in His _____ the print (_a mark_) of the nails

    b. When he put his _____ into the print of the nails

    c. When he thrust (_to insert_) his hand into His _____

65. How many days passed, after this incident (**v.26**)?

_____

66. Where were Jesus' disciples (**v.26**)?

_____

67. Who was with them (**v.26**)?

_____

68. Who came into the midst (_among_) the disciples (**v.26**)?

_____

69. What was the state of the doors this time (**v.26**)[208]?

_____

70. What did Jesus say to the disciples (**v.26**)?

_____

_____

[205] **John 20:23**: To retain means _to continue to hold onto and not dismiss_ (in this case: the sins of others)
[206] **John 20:23**: Jesus is clearly not giving the apostles the authority to remit and retain sins in order to save souls from Hell (this is never seen in Scripture), but is instead giving them authority to make judgments regarding the assembly of believers, which is His church (cf. **Matthew 16:19; 18:15-20**), in His place
[207] **John 20:24**: Didymus means _a twin_
[208] **John 20:26**: To be shut means _to be shut in order to forbid entrance to another_

71. What did He say to Thomas (**v.27**)?

      a. "Reach your _____ here and behold (*to look upon*) my

      _____..."

      b. "Reach your _____ here and thrust it into my _____..."

      c. "Be not _____..."

      d. "Be _____."

72. What was Thomas' answer to Jesus (**v.28**)?

      a. "My _____ (*Master*)..."

      b. "My _____."

73. Why did Jesus say that Thomas believed in Him (**v.29**)?

_____

74. Who did He say were blessed (**v.29**)?

_____

75. Have you ever seen Jesus Christ?

_____

76. Do you believe in Him as your Savior (**Romans 9:10-13**)?

_____

77. Does this mean that Jesus calls you more blessed than Thomas (**v.29**)?

_____

78. What else did Jesus do in the presence of His disciples (**v.30**)[209]?

_____

79. Did John write these things down in his book (**v.30**)?

_____

80. Why did John write the things that he did in his book (**v.31**)?

      a. "That you all might _____ that Jesus is the Christ (*Messiah*), the

      Son of God..."

      b. "That by _____ this, you all might have life (*eternal life*)

      through His name."

81. How does someone gain eternal life (**v.31**)?

_____

---

[209] **John 20:30**: Signs mean *miracles of authentication* (in this case: of Jesus' resurrection)

Meditation (What God Spoke to Me About):

_____
_____
_____
_____
_____
_____
_____
_____

Application (How I Can Apply What I Learned):

_____
_____
_____
_____
_____
_____
_____
_____

Memorization (How I Can Retain What I Read):

Suggestions: *John 20:1-8; 20:11-17; 20:19-23; 20:26-31*

_____
_____
_____
_____

Assessment (How I Am Doing With My Application and Memorization):

_____
_____
_____
_____
_____
_____

Bible Study Questions (*John 21:1-25*)

Instructions: Pray that God will help you to understand this passage. Read through this Bible passage twice: once for reading and another time for understanding. After reading, consider and answer the questions listed below. Write down notes regarding anything else God spoke to you about.

1. After the things mentioned in the previous chapter, what did Jesus do (*v.1*)?

_____

2. Where did He do this (*v.1*)[210] [211]?

_____

3. Who were together at the Sea of Tiberias (*v.2*)[212]?

     a. Simon _____

     b. _____, called Didymus (*a twin*)

     c. _____ of Cana in Galilee

     d. The sons of _____

     e. _____ other of Jesus' disciples (*a learner or pupil*)

4. What did Peter say to the others (*v.3*)[213]?

_____

5. What did the others say in reply (*v.3*)?

_____

6. What did they do (*v.3*)?

     a. They _____ forth

     b. They entered into a _____ immediately

7. What did they catch that night (*v.3*)?

_____

8. What happened, when the morning came (*v.4*)?

_____

9. Did the disciples know that it was Jesus (*v.4*)?

_____

---

[210] *John 21:1*: The Sea of Tiberius is *the Sea of Galilee*

[211] *John 21:1*: On this wise means "***This is how He showed Himself to His disciples***:"

[212] *John 21:2*: The sons of Zebedee were James and John (cf. *Luke 5:10*)

[213] *John 21:3* (lit.): "***I depart to go to fish***."

10. What did Jesus ask them (**v.5**)[214]?

_____

11. What was their answer (**v.5**)?

_____

12. What did Jesus tell them to do (**v.6**)?

_____

13. What did He say would happen, if they did this (**v.6**)?

_____

14. Because of Jesus' words, what did they do (**v.6**)?

    a. They _____ (*to throw*)

    b. They were not able to _____ the net for the multitude (*a great*

    number) of fish

15. Because of this miracle, who spoke up (**v.7**)[215]?

_____

16. What did he say to Peter (**v.7**)?

_____

17. What did Peter do, when he heard these words (**v.7**)?

    a. He _____ (*to gird or bind around oneself*) his fisher's coat (*a linen blouse*

    that fishermen used to wear for their work) to him

    b. He _____ (*to throw*) himself into the sea

18. Why did Peter gird his fisher's coat about him (**v.7**)[216]?

_____

19. What was the response of the other disciples (**v.8**)[217]?

    a. They _____ in a little ship

    b. They dragged the _____ with the fish

20. Why did they do this (**v.8**)?

_____

_____

[214] **John 21:5**: Children was *an affectionate title used to address another person*
[215] **John 21:7**: This disciple was the apostle John
[216] **John 21:7**: To be naked means *to be clad only in undergarments*
[217] **John 21:8**: A little ship means *a small vessel* (smaller than the boat they were on)

21. About how far were they from land (**v.8**)[218]?

_____

22. What did they see, as soon as they came to land (**v.9**)[219]?

_____

23. What was laid on it (**v.9**)?

_____

24. What did Jesus tell the disciples to do (**v.10**)?

_____

25. What did Peter do (**v.11**)?

      a. He _____ up

      b. He _____ the net to land

26. What was the state of the net (**v.11**)[220]?

_____

27. What was the number of fish they caught (**v.11**)?

_____

28. Even though the net was so full, what did not happen to it (**v.11**)?

_____

29. What did Jesus then command them to do (**v.12**)?

_____

30. What did none of the disciples ask Jesus (**v.12**)?

_____

31. Why did they not ask Him this (**v.12**)?

_____

32. What did Jesus then do (**v.13**)?

      a. He _____

      b. He _____ bread

      c. He _____ it to them

33. What did Jesus do with the fish (**v.13**)?

_____

---

[218] **John 21:8**: Two hundred cubits is *about three hundred feet* (or one hundred yards)
[219] **John 21:9**: This fire was *a heap of burning coals*
[220] **John 21:11**: Great means *large*

34. Was this the third, fourth, or fifth time that Jesus had showed Himself to His disciples, after He was risen from the dead (*v.14*)?

_____

35. What did Jesus say to Peter, after they had dined (*v.15*)[221]?

_____

36. What were the "these" that Jesus was referring to (*v.11*)?

_____

37. What was Peter's response (*v.15*)?

      a. "Yea (*Yes*), _____..."

      b. "You _____ that I love (*to be friendly toward*) you."

38. What did Jesus say in reply (*v.15*)[222] [223]?

_____

39. What did Jesus ask Peter a second time (*v.16*)[224]?

_____

40. What was Peter's reply (*v.16*)?

      a. "Yea (*Yes*), _____..."

      b. "You know that I _____ (*to be friendly toward*) you

41. What was Jesus' reply this time (*v.16*)[225] [226]?

_____

42. What did Jesus ask Peter a third time (*v.17*)[227]?

_____

43. What happened to Peter, because Jesus asked him this a third time (*v.17*)[228]?

_____

_____

[221] **John 21:15**: To love means *to have godly love toward*
[222] **John 21:15**: To feed is figurative; speaking of *the duty of a Christian teacher to teach God's Word and promote the doctrine of Christ to the church, in particular*
[223] **John 21:15**: Lamb is figurative; speaking of *the tender, more immature followers of Christ*
[224] **John 21:16**: To love means *to have godly love toward*
[225] **John 21:16**: To feed is figurative; speaking specifically of *a pastor's tending to God's flock* (His church) (not just feeding the flock)
[226] **John 21:16**: Sheep is figurative; speaking of *the more mature followers of Christ*
[227] **John 21:17**: To love means *to be friendly toward or to wish one well*
[228] **John 21:17**: To grieve means *to be in great sorrow*

44. What was his reply to Jesus (**v.17**)?

      a. "Lord, you _____ all things…"

      b. "Lord, you _____ that I love (*to be friendly toward*) you."

45. What was Jesus' reply (**v.17**)[229] [230]?

_____

46. What else did Jesus have to say to Peter (**v.18**)?

      a. "When you were _____ (*younger*), you girded (*to dress*) yourself…"

      b. "When you were _____, you walked where you would…"

      c. "When you will be _____, you will stretch forth your hands…"

      d. "When you will be _____, another will gird you…"

      e. "When you will be _____, another will carry (*to lead*) you where you

      would not."

47. Why did Jesus say this to Peter (**v.19**)?

_____

48. After He said this, what did He say to him (**v.19**)[231]?

_____

49. What did Peter then do (**v.20**)?

      a. He _____ about

      b. He saw the _____ whom Jesus loved (*the apostle John*)

50. What was this disciple doing (**v.20**)?

_____

51. What had this disciple done previously (**v.20**)[232]?

      a. He leaned (*to fall back upon*) on _____ breast at supper

      b. He asked Him, "_____, who is he that will betray you?"

52. What did Peter ask Jesus about John, when he saw him (**v.21**)?

_____

_____

[229] **John 21:17**: To feed is figurative; speaking of *the duty of a Christian teacher to teach God's Word and promote the doctrine of Christ to the church, in particular*

[230] **John 21:17**: Sheep is figurative; speaking of *mankind in general, which is in need of salvation through the Gospel*

[231] **John 21:19**: To follow means *to cleave steadfastly to one, to conform wholly to his example: in living and, if need be, in dying also* (in this case: speaking of Peter following Jesus in this way)

[232] **John 21:20**: cf. **John 13:23-25**

53. What was Jesus' answer (**v.22**)[233]?

_____

54. What did Jesus command Peter to do (**v.22**)?

_____

55. Should we be worried about how everyone else follows Jesus or about how we do (**v.22**)?

_____

56. Because of Jesus' words, what saying was there among the brethren (**v.23**)?

_____

57. What had Jesus not said to John (**v.23**)?

_____

58. What had He said instead (**v.23**)?

_____

59. Was the disciple that Jesus spoke of the one that write this Gospel record (*the book of* **John**) (**v.24**)?

_____

60. What did he say that he did (**v.24**)?

    a. He _____ (*to declare*) of these things

    b. He _____ of these things

61. What did the readers of John's testimony know about the things he wrote (**v.24**)?

_____

62. What else did Jesus do during His time on Earth (**v.25**)?

_____

63. What did John say would happen, if someone tried to write down everything Jesus did (**v.25**)?

_____

_____

64. What word did John use to close his Gospel record (**v.25**)[234]?

_____

_____

---

[233] **John 21:22** (lit.): "**If I desire that he survive until I come again, what is that to you?**"
[234] **John 21:25**: Amen means *may it be fulfilled*

Meditation (What God Spoke to Me About):

_____

_____

_____

_____

_____

_____

_____

Application (How I Can Apply What I Learned):

_____

_____

_____

_____

_____

_____

_____

_____

_____

Memorization (How I Can Retain What I Read):

Suggestions: _John 21:3-6; 21:15-17; 21:18-22; 21:25_

_____

_____

_____

Assessment (How I Am Doing With My Application and Memorization):

_____

_____

_____

_____

_____

_____

John 11-21 Answer Key

(John 11:1-57)

1. Lazarus
2. Bethany
3. Mary and Martha
4. a. Anointed b. Hair
5. He was her brother
6. They sent word unto Jesus
7. "Lord, behold, he that you love is sick."
8. "This sickness is not unto death…"
9. a. Glory b. Glorified
10. Love
11. He abode two days in the same place, where He was
12. Two days
13. "Let us go again into Judaea."
14. Master
15. a. Stone b. Go
16. a. Hours b. Stumble
17. Because he sees the light of this world
18. He stumbles
19. Because there is no light in him
20. The Light of the World
21. No
22. Darkness
23. a. Sleeps b. Wake
24. "Lord, if he sleep, he will do well."
25. Lazarus' death
26. Taking rest of sleep
27. a. Dead b. Glad
28. That His disciples might believe in Him
29. "Nevertheless, let us go to him."
30. Thomas
31. Didymus
32. "Let us also go…"
33. So they could die with Jesus
34. That Lazarus had been in the grave for four days
35. Jerusalem
36. About fifteen furlongs
37. Many of the Jews
38. To comfort them concerning their brother
39. Martha
40. a. Went b. Met
41. She continued to sit in the house
42. Lord
43. "If you had been here, my brother would not have died."
44. "That even now, whatever you will ask of God, He will give it to you."
45. "Your brother will rise again."
46. "I know that he will rise again, in the resurrection…"
47. At the last day
48. "I am the Resurrection and the Life…"
49. "Though he were dead, yet will he live…"
50. a. Lives b. Believes
51. "Do you believe this?"
52. <Personal answer>
53. <Personal answer>
54. a. Lord b. Christ
55. a. Way b. Called
56. a. Master b. Master
57. a. Arose b. Came
58. a. Town b. Martha
59. The Jews
60. Comforting Mary
61. They followed her
62. "She goes to the grave to weep there."
63. a. Saw b. Fell
64. "Lord, if you had been here, my brother would not have died."
65. a. Weeping b. Weeping
66. a. Groaned b. Troubled
67. "Where have you all laid him?"
68. "Lord, come and see."
69. He wept
70. "Behold, how He loved him!"
71. "Could not this man, which opened the eyes of the blind, have cause that even this man should not have died?"
72. a. Groaned b. Grave
73. a. Cave b. Stone
74. "You all, take away the stone."
75. a. Stinks b. Dead
76. "If you believe, you will see the glory of God…"
77. By believing in Jesus

78. They took away the stone, from the place where the dead laid

79. He lifted up His eyes

80. a. Heard b. Hear c. People

81. That the people would believe that God the Father had sent Him

82. He cried out with a loud voice

83. "Lazarus, come forth!"

84. He that was dead came forth

85. a. Hand, foot b. Face

86. a. Loose b. Go

87. They believed on Jesus

88. a. Pharisees b. Jesus

89. They gathered a council

90. "What do we do?"

91. Because He did many miracles

92. a. Believe b. Romans c. Romans

93. Caiaphas

94. The High Priest

95. a. Nothing b. Die c. Perish

96. No

97. a. Jesus b. Jesus

98. He would gather together in one the children of God that were scattered abroad

99. They took counsel to put Jesus to death

100. He did not walk openly among the Jews

101. a. Wilderness b. Ephraim

102. He continued with His disciples

103. The Jews' Passover

104. Many went out of the country up to Jerusalem, before Passover

105. To purify themselves

106. a. Sought b. Spoke

107. a. Think b. Feast

108. Both the chief priests and Pharisees

109. That if any man knew where He was, that he should show it

110. That they might take Him

(John 12:1-50)

1. He came to Bethany

2. Lazarus

3. He raised him from the dead

4. a. Supper b. Served

5. He sat at the table with Jesus

6. a. Ointment b. Anointed c. Wiped

7. It was very costly

8. It was filled with the odor of the ointment

9. Judas Iscariot

10. Simon's

11. He would betray Him

12. That it should have been sold for three hundred pence

13. That it should have been given to the poor

14. a. Poor b. Thief

15. a. Bag b. Bore

16. a. Alone b. Burying

17. The poor

18. Him

19. Much people of the Jews

20. a. Jesus' b. Lazarus

21. He raised Lazarus from the dead

22. That they might also put Lazarus to death

23. a. Away b. Believed

24. Many people came to the feast

25. They heard that Jesus was coming to Jerusalem

26. a. Palm b. Meet

27. "Hosanna! Blessed is the King of Israel that comes in the name of the Lord!"

28. A young ass (donkey)

29. "Fear not, daughter of Zion. Behold! Your King comes, sitting on an ass' colt."

30. No

31. a. Written b. Done

32. The people that were with Jesus, when Lazarus was raised from the dead

33. The people met Jesus

34. They heard that He had done that miracle

35. a. Prevail b. World

36. Certain Greeks

37. To worship at the feast

38. Philip

39. "Sir, we would see Jesus."

40. He went and told Andrew

41. They both went and told Jesus

42. The hour that the Son of Man would be glorified

43. It would abide alone

44. It brings forth much fruit

45. a. Lose b. Keep

46. "Let him follow me."

47. Where He is

48. He would honor him

49. That it was troubled

50. "Father, save me from this hour."
51. Because He came to that hour for that cause (dying)
52. "Father, glorify your name."
53. a. Glorified b. Glorify
54. a. Thundered b. Angel
55. a. Come b. Sakes
56. The judgment of the world
57. That he would be cast out
58. That He would draw all men unto Himself
59. To signify by which death He should die
60. That He abides forever
61. a. Man b. Man
62. "Yet a little while is the light with you…"
63. To walk while they had the light
64. Lest darkness came upon them
65. They do not know where they are going
66. To believe in the light
67. So that they would be the children of light
68. a. Departed b. Hid
69. They did not believe on Him
70. Isaiah
71. a. Report b. Revealed
72. They could not believe in Jesus
73. a. Blinded b. Hardened
74. a. See b. Understand
75. a. Converted b. Healed
76. a. Glory b. Spoke
77. Many believed on Jesus
78. They did not confess Him
79. a. Synagogue b. Praise, praise
80. Not on Him, but on Him that sent Jesus (God the Father)
81. They saw Him that sent Him (the Father)
82. A light
83. So that whoever believed on Him would not abide in darkness
84. That He did not judge them
85. a. Judge b. Save
86. a. Reject b. Receive
87. The word that Jesus spoke
88. Because He did not speak of Himself
89. a. Say b. Speak
90. That it is life everlasting
91. That He spoke whatever the Father told Him to say to them

(John 13:1-38)

1. a. Passover b. Hour
2. He would depart out of this world
3. To the Father
4. His own, which were in the world
5. Unto the end
6. Supper
7. He had put into Judas' heart to betray Jesus
8. a. Given b. Come c. Went
9. a. Rose b. Garments c. Towel d. Girded
10. a. Water b. Wash c. Wiped
11. Simon Peter
12. "Lord, do you wash my feet?"
13. a. Know b. Know
14. "You will never wash my feet."
15. "If I do not wash you, you have no part with me."
16. a. Feet b. Hands, head
17. a. Feet b. Clean
18. "You all are clean, but not all."
19. Because He knew who would betray Him
20. a. Garments b. Sat
21. "Do you know what I have done to you?"
22. Master and Lord
23. "You all say well…"
24. Because He was those things
25. To wash one another's feet
26. Because He gave them an example that they should do as He did to them
27. a. Servant b. Sent
28. That they would be happy
29. No
30. He knew who He had chosen
31. "He that eats bread with me has lifted up his heel against me."
32. So that, when it came to pass, they would believe in Jesus
33. That they receive Him (Jesus)
34. That they receive Him that sent Jesus
35. a. Troubled b. Testified
36. "One of you will betray me."
37. a. Looked b. Doubted
38. One of Jesus' disciples, whom He loved
39. Simon Peter
40. That he should ask Jesus of whom He spoke
41. a. Jesus' b. Lord

42. "It is he to whom I will give a sop, when I have dipped it."

43. Judas Iscariot

44. Satan entered into him

45. "That which you will do, do quickly."

46. No

47. a. Buy b. Poor

48. Because Judas had the bag

49. He went immediately out

50. It was night

51. a. Glorified b. Glorified

52. a. Glorify b. Glorify

53. Little children

54. That He would be with them yet a little while

55. That they would seek Him

56. "To where I go, you all cannot come."

57. A new commandment

58. a. Love, loved b. Love

59. If they had love one to another

60. If we love one another

61. Simon Peter

62. "Lord, to where do you go?"

63. a. Follow b. Follow

64. "Why can I not follow you now?"

65. Lay down his life for Jesus' sake

66. "Will you lay down your life for my sake?"

67. That the cock would not crow, until Peter had denied Jesus thrice

(John 14:1-31)

1. To not let their hearts be troubled

2. Believe also in Him (Jesus)

3. Many mansions

4. If it were not so

5. To prepare a place for them

6. a. Come b. Receive

7. So that where He is, we can be also

8. a. Know b. Know

9. Thomas

10. a. Know b. Know

11. a. Way b. Truth c. Life

12. He cannot, unless he goes through Jesus

13. The only way

14. He cannot

15. His Father (God) also

16. a. Know b. Seen

17. Philip

18. a. Show b. Suffices

19. a. Time b. Known

20. The Father

21. "How do you then say, 'Show us the Father.'?"

22. a. Believe b. Believe

23. That He did not speak of Himself, but the Father

24. The Father that dwelled in Jesus

25. a. Father b. Father

26. For the very works' sake

27. a. Works b. Works

28. Because Jesus went to His Father

29. That whatever they asked in Jesus' name, He would do

30. So that the Father may be glorified in the Son

31. "If you all ask anything in my name, I will do it."

32. Asking in the name of Jesus

33. Keep His commandments

34. To pray to the Father

35. That He would give them another Comforter

36. That He would abide with them forever

37. The Spirit of Truth

38. The world cannot receive Him

39. a. See b. Know

40. "You all know Him…"

41. a. Dwelled b. In

42. a. Comfortless b. Come

43. a. See b. See

44. They would live also

45. a. Father b. Him (Jesus) c. He

46. a. Have b. Keep

47. a. Loved b. Love c. Manifest

48. Judas

49. No

50. "Lord, how is it that you will manifest yourself to us and not to the world?"

51. "If a man love me, he will keep my words…"

52. a. Father b. Come c. Abode

53. That they do not keep His sayings

54. Not His, but the Father's, which sent Him

55. Yes

56. The Comforter

57. The Holy Ghost

58. The Father

59. He will be sent in the name of Jesus

60. a. Teach b. Bring

61. Whatever Jesus had told them

62. Peace

63. His peace

64. No

65. "Let not your hearts be troubled, neither let it be afraid."

66. a. Go b. Come

67. They would rejoice, because of the things He said

68. a. Father b. Father

69. So that, when it came to pass, they would believe

70. That He would not talk much with them

71. a. Prince b. Prince

72. a. Father b. Father

73. a. Arise b. Go

(John 15:1-27)

1. The True Vine

2. The Husbandmen

3. He takes it away

4. He purges it

5. So that it may bring forth more fruit

6. Through the word that Jesus had spoken to them

7. a. Abide b. Abide

8. It cannot, unless it abides in the vine

9. As we abide in Him

10. No

11. No

12. The Vine

13. The Branches

14. It brings forth much fruit

15. Because without Jesus we can do nothing

16. a. Cast b. Withered

17. a. Gather b. Fire c. Burn

18. Figuratively

19. a. Ask b. Done

20. When we bear much fruit

21. His disciples

22. His love

23. His love

24. To continue in His love

25. We can, if we keep His commandments

26. a. Kept b. Love

27. a. Joy b. Joy

28. That they love one another

29. Because He loved them

30. That a man lay down his life for his friends

31. His friends

32. If they did whatever Jesus commanded them

33. Servants

34. Because the servant does not know what his lord does

35. Friends

36. Because He had told them everything He had heard of the Father

37. No

38. a. Chosen b. Ordained

39. a. Go b. Fruit c. Fruit

40. So that whatever they asked of the Father in Jesus' name, He would give to them

41. In the name of Jesus

42. He will answer our prayers

43. No

44. No

45. So that they would love one another

46. That it hated Jesus, before it hated them

47. That the world would love its own

48. a. World b. World

49. The word that He had said to them

50. "The servant is not greater than his lord."

51. It would also persecute them

52. That it would also keep theirs

53. Yes

54. a. Name's b. Know

55. a. Came b. Spoke

56. A cloak for their sin

57. That they hate His Father also

58. The works that no other man did

59. No

60. That they had sin

61. a. Seen b. Hated

62. So that the word might be fulfilled

63. In the Jews' law

64. "They hated me without a cause."

65. The Comforter

66. Jesus

67. The Spirit of Truth

68. The Father

69. He would testify of Jesus

70. They would bear witness

71. Because they had been with Jesus from the beginning

(John 16:1-33)

1. So that they would not be offended
2. They would be put out of the synagogues
3. The time when whoever killed them would think that he was doing God a service
4. a. Known b. Known
5. So that, when the time came, they would remember that He told the disciples of them
6. Because He was with them
7. Go His way
8. To Him that sent Jesus
9. "To where do you go?"
10. Sorrow filled their hearts
11. The truth
12. That it was expedient for them that He go away
13. Because if He did not go away, the Comforter would not come to them
14. Jesus would send the Comforter to them
15. a. Sin b. Righteousness c. Judgment
16. Because they do not believe in Jesus
17. a. Father b. See
18. Because the prince of this world was judged
19. He had many things to say
20. They could not bear them
21. The Spirit of Truth
22. The Comforter
23. He would guide them into all truth
24. Because He would not speak of Himself
25. a. Speak b. Show
26. He would glorify Jesus
27. a. Receive b. Show
28. "All things that the Father has are mine."
29. Everything
30. a. Take b. Show
31. That they would not see Him
32. That they would see Him
33. Because He went to the Father
34. "What is this that He says to us?"
35. a. See b. See c. Go
36. "What is this that He says?"
37. "A little while..."
38. "We cannot tell what He says."
39. That they were desirous to ask Him
40. "Do you all inquire among yourselves of what I said?"
41. a. See b. See
42. a. Weep b. Lament
43. Rejoice
44. Their sorrow would be turned to joy
45. She has sorrow
46. Because her hour is come
47. She does not remember the anguish anymore
48. Because of joy that a man is born into the world
49. Sorrow
50. a. See b. Rejoice c. Joy
51. That they would ask Him nothing
52. That He would give it to them
53. We pray through Jesus
54. No
55. a. Ask b. Receive
56. So that their joy would be full
57. Proverbs
58. a. Proverbs b. Plainly
59. That they would ask in Jesus' name
60. Pray to the Father for them
61. Because the Father Himself loved them
62. a. Loved b. Believed
63. a. Father b. World c. World d. Father
64. a. Plainly b. Proverb
65. a. Know b. Ask
66. That Jesus came forth from God
67. "Do you all now believe?"
68. a. Scattered b. Alone
69. Every man would go to his own
70. "Yet I am not alone."
71. Because the Father was with Him
72. So that they might have peace in Him
73. Jesus
74. Tribulation
75. To be of good cheer
76. Because Jesus overcame the world
77. <Personal answer>
78. <Personal answer>

(John 17:1-26)

1. He lifted His eyes to Heaven
2. a. Hour b. Glorify
3. So that He also would glorify the Father
4. Power over all flesh
5. So that Jesus could give eternal life to as many as God had given Him
6. a. Know b. Know
7. Jesus Christ

8. a. Glorified b. Finished
9. To glorify Him
10. For the Father to glorify Him
11. Since before the world was
12. He manifested the Father's name
13. To the men God gave Him from out of the world
14. a. They b. Gave c. Kept
15. That all things whatsoever the Father had given Jesus were from the Father
16. a. Given, given b. Received c. Came d. Sent
17. Them (those that God had given Him)
18. a. World b. Given
19. a. They b. All c. All d. Glorified
20. That He was not more in the world
21. That they were in the world
22. Coming to the Father
23. "Holy Father"
24. "Keep through your own name those that you have given me."
25. So that they would be one, as the Father and Son are one
26. To be one in Christ
27. He kept them in the Father's name
28. a. Kept b. Lost
29. The Son of Perdition
30. So that the scripture would be fulfilled
31. a. Come b. Speak
32. So that His disciples might have His joy fulfilled in themselves
33. God's word
34. The world hated them
35. Because the disciples were not of this world
36. Because Jesus was not of this world
37. a. World b. Keep
38. That they were not of the world
39. That He was not of the world
40. To sanctify them
41. Through God's truth
42. God's Word
43. Sent Him into the world
44. Sent them into the world
45. He sanctified Himself
46. So that the disciples might be sanctified through the truth
47. Through God's truth
48. a. Alone b. Believe

49. <Personal answer>
50. <Personal answer>
51. So that they all may be one
52. a. One b. Believe
53. a. Father b. Son
54. The glory that God had given Him
55. So that they may be one
56. They are united
57. United
58. a. Jesus b. Father
59. a. Perfect b. World c. World
60. As much as He loves the Son
61. That they would be with Him, where He was
62. So that they may behold Jesus' glory
63. The Father
64. Because the Father loved the Son before the foundation of the world
65. "Righteous Father"
66. That it did not know the Father
67. That He had known the Father
68. a. Knew b. Declared
69. Declare the name of the Father
70. a. Love, loved b. In

(John 18:1-40)

1. They went forth over the brook Cedron
2. A garden
3. They entered into it
4. Judas
5. Betray Him (Jesus)
6. Jesus often resorted there with His disciples
7. a. Men b. Officers
8. a. Priests b. Pharisees
9. a. Lanterns b. Torches c. Weapons
10. All things that should come upon Him
11. He went forth
12. "Who do you all seek?"
13. "Jesus of Nazareth."
14. "I am He."
15. Judas
16. a. Backward b. Fell
17. "Who do you all seek?"
18. "Jesus of Nazareth."
19. "I have told you that I am He."
20. "Let these go their way."
21. So that the saying might be fulfilled
22. "Of them that you gave me, I have lost none."

23. Simon Peter
24. a. Drew b. Smote c. Ear
25. Malchus
26. "Put up your sword into the sheath."
27. "Will I not drink it?"
28. a. Took b. Bound c. Led
29. Annas
30. Caiaphas
31. High Priest
32. He gave counsel to the Jews
33. That it was expedient that one man should die for the people
34. a. Peter b. Disciple
35. a. Known b. Jesus
36. He stood at the door without
37. a. Out b. Spoke c. Peter
38. The damsel that kept the door
39. "Are you not also one of this man's disciples?"
40. "I am not."
41. a. Servants b. Officers
42. They had made a fire of coals
43. Because it was cold
44. They warmed themselves
45. a. Stood b. Warmed
46. The high priest
47. a. Disciples b. Doctrine
48. "I spoke openly to the world."
49. a. Synagogue b. Temple
50. The Jews resort there
51. Nothing
52. "Why do you ask me?"
53. "Ask them which heard me, what I have said to them."
54. Because they knew what Jesus had said
55. One of the officers, which stood by, struck Jesus
56. The palm of his hand
57. "Do you answer the high priest so?"
58. a. Evil, evil b. Well
59. Annas
60. Caiaphas
61. a. Stood b. Warmed
62. "Are you not also one of His disciples?"
63. He denied it
64. "I am not."
65. a. Servants b. Kinsman
66. "Did I not see you in the garden with Him?"

67. He denied it
68. The cock crew
69. To the hall of judgment
70. Early
71. No
72. a. Defiled b. Passover
73. Pilate
74. "What accusation do you all bring against this man?"
75. "If he were not a malefactor, we would not have delivered Him up to you."
76. a. Take b. Judge
77. "It is not lawful for us to put any man to death."
78. That the saying of Jesus might be fulfilled
79. He signified by what death He should die
80. a. Entered b. Called
81. "Are you the King of the Jews?"
82. a. Say b. Tell
83. "Am I a Jew?"
84. a. Nation b. Priests
85. "What have you done?"
86. "My kingdom is not of this world."
87. His servants would fight
88. So that He would not be delivered to the Jews
89. "Not from here…"
90. "Are you a king then?"
91. "You say that I am a king."
92. To this end (His death)
93. That He should bear witness unto the truth
94. Every one of them that hears Jesus' voice
95. "What is truth?"
96. He went out again to the Jews
97. "I find no fault in Him at all."
98. A custom
99. That Pilate would release a prisoner to them at Passover
100. "Will you all therefore that I should release to you the King of the Jews?"
101. "Not the man, but Barabbas!"
102. A robber

(John 19:1-42)

1. a. Took b. Scourged
2. a. Platted b. Head c. Robe
3. "Hail! King of the Jews!"
4. They smote Him with their hands
5. He went forth again

6. "Behold, I bring Him forth to you…"
7. So that they would know that he found no fault in Jesus
8. Jesus
9. a. Crown b. Purple
10. "Behold, the man!"
11. a. Priests b. Officers
12. "Crucify Him!"
13. a. Take b. Crucify
14. Because he found no fault with Jesus
15. a. Law b. Law
16. Because He made Himself the Son of God
17. He was the more afraid
18. He went again into the judgment hall
19. "From where are you?"
20. He gave him none
21. a. Speak b. Crucify c. Release
22. "You could have no power at all against me, except it were given to you from above."
23. Those that delivered Jesus to Pilate
24. Release Jesus
25. "If you let this man go, you are not Caesar's friend!"
26. That they speak against Caesar
27. a. Brought b. Judgment
28. The Pavement
29. Gabbatha
30. a. Preparation b. Sixth
31. "Behold, your king!"
32. a. Away b. Away c. Crucify
33. "Shall I crucify your king?"
34. "We have no king, but Caesar."
35. He delivered Jesus to them to be crucified
36. a. Took b. Led
37. a. Cross b. Skull
38. Golgotha
39. They crucified Him
40. Two
41. a. Side b. Midst
42. a. Wrote b. Cross
43. "Jesus of Nazareth: King of the Jews"
44. Many of the Jews
45. Because the place where Jesus was crucified was nigh to the city
46. In Hebrew, Greek, and Latin
47. a. King b. King

48. "What I have written, I have written."
49. a. Garments b. Four
50. So every soldier had a part
51. Jesus' coat
52. a. Seam b. Woven
53. a. Rend b. Cast
54. So that the scripture might be fulfilled
55. a. Parted b. Vesture
56. Yes
57. a. Mother b. Mary c. Mary
58. a. Mother b. Disciple
59. "Woman, behold your son!"
60. "Behold, your mother!"
61. He took Mary to his own home
62. That all things were accomplished
63. "I thirst."
64. So that the scripture might be fulfilled
65. A vessel full of vinegar
66. a. Sponge b. Hyssop c. Mouth
67. "It is finished."
68. a. Bowed b. Ghost
69. They besought Pilate
70. a. Legs b. Taken
71. a. Preparation b. Sabbath
72. Because that Sabbath day was a high day
73. a. Came b. Broke
74. That He was dead already
75. No
76. He pierced Jesus' side
77. A spear
78. Blood and water came out
79. He bore record
80. His record is true
81. That he said truth
82. So that the reader might believe
83. So that the scripture should be fulfilled
84. "A bone of Him will not be broken."
85. "They will look on Him whom they pierced."
86. Joseph of Arimathaea
87. He was a disciple of Jesus
88. A secret disciple
89. Because he feared the Jews
90. That he might take away the body of Jesus
91. He gave him leave
92. a. Came b. Took
93. Nicodemus

94. He came to Jesus by night
95. A mixture of myrrh and aloes
96. About one hundred pounds
97. a. Took b. Wound
98. Because it was done after the manner of the Jews is to bury
99. A garden
100. A new sepulcher
101. A man had never been laid therein
102. a. Preparation b. Sepulcher

(John 20:1-31)

1. Mary Magdalene
2. Early, when it was yet dark
3. The stone taken away from the sepulcher
4. a. Ran b. Came
5. a. Taken b. Laid
6. a. Went b. Came
7. They both ran together
8. The other disciple (John) outran Peter
9. a. Stooped b. Looked
10. He saw the linen clothes lying
11. No
12. Simon Peter
13. a. Into b. Saw c. Napkin
14. a. Clothes b. Wrapped
15. The other disciple (John)
16. a. Saw b. Believed
17. The scripture
18. That He must rise again from the dead
19. They went away again unto their own homes
20. Mary Magdalene
21. She stood outside weeping
22. a. Stooped b. Looked
23. Two angels
24. White
25. a. Head b. Feet
26. Where the body of Jesus had lain
27. "Woman, why do you weep?"
28. a. Taken b. Laid
29. a. Turned b. Jesus
30. No
31. a. Weep b. Seek
32. The gardener
33. a. Laid b. Take
34. "Mary."
35. She turned herself
36. "Rabboni!"
37. Master
38. "Touch me not."
39. Because He was not yet ascended to His Father
40. To go to His brethren
41. a. Ascend b. Ascend
42. His God and their God
43. a. Came b. Told c. Told
44. a. Came b. Stood
45. At evening
46. The first day of the week (Sunday)
47. They were shut
48. Because the feared the Jews
49. "Peace be unto you."
50. a. Hands b. Side
51. They were glad
52. "Peace be unto you."
53. He had sent Jesus
54. Jesus sent His disciples
55. He breathed on them
56. "You all, receive the Holy Ghost."
57. That their sins were remitted
58. That their sins were retained
59. Thomas
60. He was one of the twelve
61. Didymus
62. "We have seen the Lord."
63. Believe
64. a. Hands b. Finger c. Side
65. Eight days
66. They were within
67. Thomas
68. Jesus
69. They were shut
70. "Peace be unto you."
71. a. Finger, hands b. Hand, side c. Faithless d. Believing
72. a. Lord b. God
73. Because Thomas saw Him
74. Those that have not seen Jesus and yet have believed in Him
75. <Personal answer>
76. <Personal answer>
77. Yes
78. Many other signs

79. No
80. a. Believe b. Believing
81. By believing that Jesus is the Christ, the Son of God

(John 21:1-25)

1. He showed Himself again to the disciples
2. At the Sea of Tiberias
3. a. Peter b. Thomas c. Nathanael d. Zebedee e. Two
4. "I go a fishing."
5. "We also go with you."
6. a. Went b. Ship
7. Nothing
8. Jesus stood on the shore
9. No
10. "Children, have you all any meat?"
11. "No."
12. "Cast the net on the right side of the ship."
13. That they would find fish
14. a. Cast b. Draw
15. That disciple whom Jesus loved
16. "It is the Lord."
17. a. Girt b. Cast
18. Because he was naked
19. a. Came b. Net
20. Because they were not far from land
21. About two hundred cubits
22. A fire of coals
23. Fish and bread
24. "Bring of the fish, which you all have now caught."
25. a. Went b. Drew
26. It was full of great fish
27. One hundred fifty-three
28. It was not broken
29. "Come and dine."
30. "Who are you?"
31. Because they knew that it was the Lord
32. a. Came b. Took c. Gave
33. The same thing
34. The third time
35. "Simon, son of Jonas, do you love me, more than these?"
36. The fish
37. a. Lord b. Know
38. "Feed my lambs."
39. "Simon, son of Jonas, do you love me?"
40. a. Lord b. Love
41. "Feed my sheep."
42. "Simon, son of Jonas, do you love me?"
43. He was grieved
44. a. Know b. Know
45. "Feed my sheep."
46. a. Young b. Young c. Old d. Old e. Old
47. To signify by what death Peter should glorify God
48. "Follow me."
49. a. Turned b. Disciple
50. He was following
51. a. Jesus' b. Lord
52. "Lord, what will this man do?"
53. "If I will that he tarry until I come, what is that to you?"
54. You follow me."
55. About how we follow Jesus
56. That John would not die
57. That he would not die
58. "If I will that he tarry until I come, what is that to you?"
59. Yes
60. a. Testified b. Wrote
61. That his testimony is true
62. Many other things
63. The world itself could not contain the book that would be written
64. Amen

CPSIA information can be obtained
at www.ICGtesting.com
Printed in the USA
LVOW03s1431040416

482082LV00044B/1073/P